ONE

INTRODUCTION

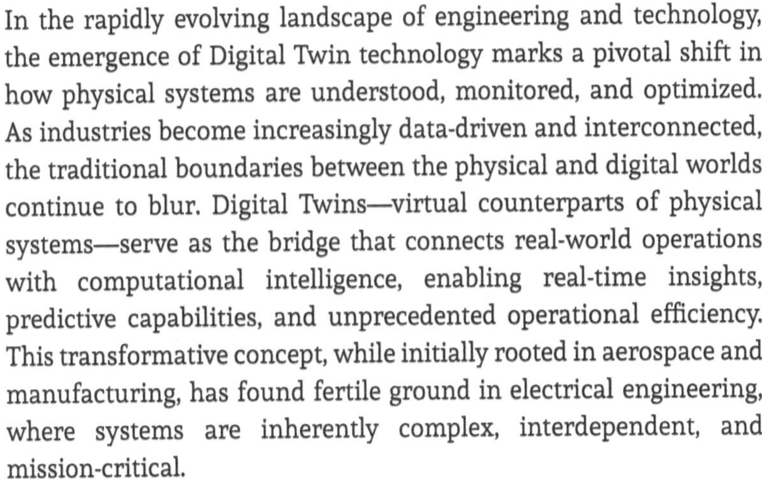

In the rapidly evolving landscape of engineering and technology, the emergence of Digital Twin technology marks a pivotal shift in how physical systems are understood, monitored, and optimized. As industries become increasingly data-driven and interconnected, the traditional boundaries between the physical and digital worlds continue to blur. Digital Twins—virtual counterparts of physical systems—serve as the bridge that connects real-world operations with computational intelligence, enabling real-time insights, predictive capabilities, and unprecedented operational efficiency. This transformative concept, while initially rooted in aerospace and manufacturing, has found fertile ground in electrical engineering, where systems are inherently complex, interdependent, and mission-critical.

A Digital Twin is more than just a digital model. It is a dynamic, living entity that continuously evolves based on real-time data from its physical counterpart. Unlike static simulations, Digital Twins are synchronized with live data streams, allowing engineers to monitor system behavior, predict failures, optimize performance, and test "what-if" scenarios in a risk-free virtual environment. In electrical engineering, where components like transformers, switchgear, motors, and power grids are expected to perform flawlessly under demanding conditions, the ability to mirror these assets digitally provides significant operational and strategic advantages. From fault detection in high-voltage equipment to energy optimization in smart buildings, Digital Twins empower engineers to make informed decisions that were previously constrained by physical limitations.

The concept of Digital Twins is not entirely new. Engineers have long relied on models and simulations to represent systems virtually. However, the convergence of key technologies—such as Internet of Things (IoT), artificial intelligence (AI), machine learning (ML), big data analytics, and cloud computing—has breathed new life into the idea, turning it from theory into practice. Today, we can create highly detailed, sensor-rich models of real systems, connect them through secure networks, and harness vast computational power to analyze and act upon data in real time. This technological evolution has brought Digital Twins out of research labs and into the heart of industries, including power generation, transmission, distribution, and renewable energy systems.

Electrical engineering, in particular, is poised to benefit immensely from the implementation of Digital Twin technology. The field is characterized by its reliance on reliability, safety, and efficiency. Electrical infrastructure must be maintained proactively, yet traditional approaches often rely on periodic inspection and fixed maintenance schedules. These methods can lead to unnecessary downtime or catastrophic failures. Digital Twins offer a paradigm shift, enabling condition-based and predictive maintenance strategies that are tailored to the actual state of the asset. This leads to reduced operational costs, increased asset longevity, and improved system availability. Moreover, by simulating the impact of control strategies and environmental changes in a virtual environment, Digital Twins enhance system design and optimization, ensuring that engineering decisions are both data-informed and forward-looking.

Beyond operations and maintenance, Digital Twins serve a strategic role in planning and innovation. In grid modernization projects, for example, utility companies can use Digital Twins to model the integration of distributed energy resources, simulate

DIGITAL TWIN IN ELECTRICAL ENGINEERING: FROM CONCEPT TO IMPLEMENTATION

P.VINODH KUMAR

S.NANDAKUMAR

B.VASANTHAN

S.GUNASEKARAN

Contents

demand response strategies, and assess the resilience of the grid under various stress scenarios. In electric vehicle infrastructure, they help evaluate charging station performance and network impact. In industrial automation, they enable seamless virtual commissioning of control systems, thereby reducing commissioning time and cost. These examples illustrate that the potential applications are not only diverse but also deeply transformative, reshaping how electrical engineers approach both problems and solutions.

Despite the evident benefits, the journey to implement Digital Twins is not without its challenges. High upfront investment in sensors, connectivity, and computational infrastructure can be a barrier for some organizations. The success of a Digital Twin depends heavily on the quality, granularity, and timeliness of data collected from the physical system. Data integration across heterogeneous sources, interoperability with legacy systems, and ensuring cybersecurity are all complex tasks that require careful planning and execution. Additionally, creating accurate and adaptable models that can represent real-world behavior under diverse conditions remains a significant technical challenge. These hurdles, while non-trivial, are surmountable with the right strategy, tools, and expertise.

Education and workforce readiness also play a vital role in the broader adoption of Digital Twin technology. Electrical engineers must now be equipped not only with domain-specific knowledge but also with skills in data analytics, systems modeling, AI, and digital communication protocols. The engineering curriculum must evolve to include these interdisciplinary capabilities, ensuring that the next generation of engineers can thrive in a digitally transformed environment. Universities and research institutions are already beginning to introduce Digital Twin platforms in labs and projects, fostering innovation and practical experience.

This book was written in response to the growing interest and urgent need for a comprehensive, practice-oriented resource on Digital Twin technology in electrical engineering. While academic literature and technical reports provide isolated insights, there is a lack of integrated material that connects theory with hands-on application. This book aims to fill that gap by guiding readers through the foundational concepts, enabling technologies, architectural components, and real-world implementation strategies of Digital Twins. It offers both breadth and depth, from an introductory understanding to advanced techniques used in industrial environments. Through case studies, diagrams, and project examples, it ensures that the reader gains not only conceptual clarity but also practical confidence.

Whether you are a student beginning your journey in electrical engineering, a seasoned professional seeking to modernize operations, or a researcher exploring new frontiers in cyber-physical systems, this book serves as a roadmap. It equips you with the tools to understand the mechanics of Digital Twins, appreciate their value, and ultimately apply them to create smarter, safer, and more sustainable electrical systems. As we stand at the crossroads of digital innovation and engineering practice, mastering the art of Digital Twins is not just an opportunity—it is a necessity.

The road ahead is filled with potential. As technology continues to evolve, the capabilities of Digital Twins will only expand, becoming more intelligent, autonomous, and interconnected. Their integration with emerging technologies such as augmented reality (AR), virtual reality (VR), blockchain, and 5G will open new dimensions in how we interact with and control our electrical infrastructure. We are only scratching the surface of what's possible. Through this book, you will gain the insight to not only follow this transformation but to be an active participant in shaping the future of electrical engineering in the digital age.

TWO
FOUNDATIONS OF DIGITAL TWIN

As we step deeper into the digital transformation of engineering systems, understanding the foundational principles of Digital Twin technology becomes critical. Digital Twins are more than digital copies—they are sophisticated, intelligent, and interactive systems that mirror the state, behavior, and functionality of physical entities. Their development and integration mark a new chapter in how engineers design, monitor, and optimize real-world processes. Before we explore specific applications in electrical engineering, it is essential to examine the core elements that constitute a Digital Twin: the components, technologies, and conceptual underpinnings that enable this powerful convergence of the physical and digital worlds.

The essence of a Digital Twin lies in its ability to maintain an active, real-time connection with its physical counterpart. This bi-directional linkage is established through a combination of sensing, communication, data integration, modeling, and analytics. Each layer of this architecture plays a critical role in ensuring that the digital representation remains synchronized with reality, not just passively reflecting the system's state, but also predicting and prescribing future actions. A true Digital Twin is, therefore, dynamic and evolving—it updates as new data flows in, learns from historical behavior, and adapts to new inputs, ultimately forming the basis for autonomous decision-making in complex engineering environments.

The foundational architecture of a Digital Twin can be visualized as a layered system. At the base lies the physical asset—a machine, component, system, or process that needs to be modeled. This asset is embedded with sensors and data acquisition devices that collect a variety of parameters such as temperature, voltage, current, speed, vibration, humidity, and more. The role of sensors is paramount—they serve as the eyes and ears of the Digital Twin, feeding it with the data necessary for accurate modeling. This data must then be transmitted through a robust communication infrastructure that ensures low-latency, high-bandwidth, and secure data exchange. Protocols such as MQTT, OPC UA, Modbus, and IEC 61850 are frequently used depending on the nature and domain of the application.

Once the data is acquired and transmitted, it arrives at the data integration and storage layer, where it is cleaned, formatted, and made available for processing. This is typically handled by edge devices or cloud-based systems, which provide the computational resources necessary for storing historical data and executing analytical operations. Here, real-time processing and batch analytics work in tandem to provide both immediate responses and long-term insights. The Digital Twin now requires a model that can accurately simulate and predict the behavior of the physical system. This model may be physics-based, relying on first-principle equations and differential modeling, or data-driven, built using machine learning algorithms trained on historical operational data. In many cases, a hybrid modeling approach is adopted, combining the strengths of both paradigms to deliver accurate, interpretable, and scalable results.

One of the distinguishing features of Digital Twin technology is its ability to go beyond simple monitoring to support predictive and prescriptive analytics. By analyzing trends and detecting anomalies, Digital Twins can forecast future system states and recommend corrective actions before issues arise. In electrical systems, this could mean identifying a slowly degrading insulation in a motor, anticipating transformer overload conditions, or predicting harmonic distortion in power converters. The application of AI and ML techniques—such as decision trees, neural networks, support vector machines, and reinforcement learning—enables the Digital Twin to evolve into an intelligent entity capable of autonomous behavior, self-correction, and continuous optimization.

Interactivity is another core aspect of Digital Twin foundations. Engineers and operators must be able to interface with the digital model through visualization tools, dashboards, and human-machine interfaces (HMIs). These platforms allow for real-time inspection, remote diagnostics, and virtual experimentation. In modern environments, these tools are often enhanced with augmented or virtual reality, enabling immersive interaction with the Digital Twin. This is particularly valuable in training scenarios, safety assessments, or when dealing with complex electrical systems that are hazardous to access physically.

Beyond the technical components, it is important to understand the systemic nature of Digital Twins. A Digital Twin is not created in isolation—it exists as part of a larger cyber-physical system where multiple digital models interact with one another and with external control systems. In power systems, for example, a Digital Twin of a substation must coordinate with those of feeders, transformers, generators, and control units. This requires semantic interoperability and standardization in how data is exchanged and interpreted. The concept of the Digital Thread complements the Digital Twin by providing a unified data flow across the asset's lifecycle—from design and manufacturing to operation and retirement—ensuring continuity and traceability.

Foundational technologies that support the development of Digital Twins include a wide range of digital innovations. IoT platforms provide sensor connectivity and data management. Cloud computing offers scalable storage and processing capabilities. Edge computing supports low-latency, decentralized data handling, particularly important for real-time control in electrical systems. Big data technologies facilitate the handling of high-volume and high-velocity data streams. Artificial intelligence provides cognitive capabilities for pattern recognition, decision-making, and continuous learning. Together, these technologies form the backbone of the Digital Twin ecosystem, enabling it to deliver on its promise of intelligence, efficiency, and resilience.

Security is a foundational concern that cannot be overlooked. As Digital Twins involve continuous data exchange and often control critical infrastructure, ensuring cybersecurity is vital. Measures must be taken to protect data integrity, prevent unauthorized access, and ensure system resilience against cyberattacks. Techniques such as encryption, access control, anomaly detection, and blockchain-based authentication are increasingly being integrated into Digital Twin frameworks to address these concerns.

Understanding the foundational concepts of Digital Twin technology is essential for any successful implementation. This includes not only the technical architecture but also the philosophy and mindset behind it. At its heart, a Digital Twin is about enhancing visibility, insight, and control. It enables engineers to move from reactive responses to proactive strategies. It shifts design thinking from static blueprints to dynamic systems. It transforms maintenance from scheduled routines to intelligent decisions. By embedding intelligence into every layer of a system's operation, the Digital Twin redefines what it means to manage electrical assets in a digital era.

As we continue through this book, the foundation laid in this chapter will serve as the springboard for deeper exploration. We will see how these concepts translate into real-world electrical engineering systems—from power generation and distribution networks to electric machines and smart buildings. The journey ahead will illustrate that mastering the foundations of Digital Twin technology is not just about understanding components and architectures—it is about embracing a new way of engineering that is data-rich, intelligence-driven, and future-ready.

THREE

CORE COMPONENTS

Physical System

The Physical System forms the core foundation of any Digital Twin implementation. It is the actual, tangible entity in the real world that the digital model aims to replicate, understand, and control. In essence, the Digital Twin is built around this physical system—observing it, learning from it, and optimizing it. This could include individual electrical components, entire subsystems, or large-scale infrastructure. In electrical engineering, physical systems often include both stationary and dynamic equipment used across generation, transmission, distribution, and consumption of electrical energy.

Examples in Electrical Engineering

- Transformer in a Substation: One of the most critical components in power distribution. Monitoring its oil temperature, insulation health, load conditions, and harmonic levels is essential. A Digital Twin can help predict transformer aging or overheating before it causes failure.
- Industrial Motor or Drive: Motors are widely used in factories and automation setups. Tracking torque, speed, vibration, current draw, and temperature allows for early detection of

bearing wear or misalignment.

- Entire Power Distribution Network: In smart grids, feeders, switchgear, relays, and meters form a complex system. The physical system here consists of multiple interconnected components working under varying loads and environmental conditions.
- Solar Panel Array or Wind Turbine: Renewable energy systems are ideal for Digital Twin applications. For instance, turbine blade stress levels, generator output, and wind speed can be tracked in real-time to improve efficiency and reliability.
- Smart Home Electrical Grid: Smart homes feature smart meters, IoT-enabled appliances, lighting systems, and battery storage units. All of these components form a physical system whose performance can be optimized using a Digital Twin for better energy management.

Sensor Integration and Data Acquisition

The physical system is not just a passive entity—it is actively instrumented with a wide range of smart sensors, actuators, and embedded controllers. These devices continuously monitor various operational parameters and send this data to the digital layer. For electrical systems, common sensor types include:

- Voltage sensors: Monitor line voltages and voltage drops.
- Current transformers (CTs): Track current flow and power usage.
- Temperature sensors: Detect overheating in equipment like cables, motors, and switchgear.
- Vibration sensors: Identify mechanical imbalance or motor misalignment.
- Pressure and humidity sensors: Important for sealed electrical environments or enclosures.
- Hall effect sensors: Measure magnetic field strength, often used in motors or switchgear.

The collected data is processed by microcontrollers or programmable logic controllers (PLCs) before being transmitted to higher-level systems for analysis. The accuracy, frequency, and granularity of this sensor data directly influence the performance of the Digital Twin.

Bi-directional Communication

In traditional systems, data flows in one direction—from the machine to the monitoring system. However, in a Digital Twin-enabled environment, the physical system supports bi-directional communication. This capability allows the digital model to not only *observe* the system but also to *interact* with it in meaningful ways.

For example:

- A Digital Twin of a circuit breaker might detect abnormal switching patterns and send control commands to reset or reconfigure it.
- In a smart grid, a Digital Twin could dynamically change load-sharing between substations based on real-time demand forecasts.
- An electric motor's Digital Twin might recommend operational changes or even trigger automatic shutdown to prevent a failure.

Bi-directional communication is typically enabled via industrial communication protocols such as:

- Modbus/TCP
- OPC-UA
- IEC 61850 (specific to substation automation)
- MQTT (widely used in IoT applications)

These protocols allow for secure, scalable, and reliable data transmission between the physical and digital layers.

Role in Lifecycle Management

The physical system's role extends across the entire lifecycle of an asset—from design and commissioning to operation, maintenance, and decommissioning. With a Digital Twin in place, engineers can track how the system behaves under different conditions over time. This leads to improved:

- Predictive Maintenance: By identifying wear-and-tear patterns early, costly breakdowns can be avoided.
- Performance Optimization: Adjustments in real time based on usage patterns can enhance energy efficiency.
- Design Feedback: Insights from real-world performance feed back into the design of the next generation of products or systems.

Challenges and Considerations

Implementing a Digital Twin for a physical system comes with certain challenges:

- Sensor Cost and Placement: Choosing the right type and number of sensors while keeping costs in check is crucial.
- Environmental Constraints: Electrical environments may have electromagnetic interference, heat, or moisture, which can affect sensor accuracy.
- Data Synchronization: Ensuring the timing of data across multiple sensors is accurate and consistent.
- Scalability: As systems grow, so does the need for scalable sensor networks and data management.

The physical system is the heartbeat of a Digital Twin—it is where the journey begins. By embedding intelligence at the physical level and enabling real-time communication with the digital world, organizations unlock new levels of visibility, performance, and control. As electrical systems become more complex and interdependent, the role of well-instrumented, communicative, and analyzable physical systems becomes indispensable in the creation of effective and transformative Digital Twins.

DIGITAL MODEL

The Digital Model is the central and most intelligent part of the Digital Twin system. It is a virtual counterpart that mirrors the behavior, structure, and performance of the physical system using mathematical models, algorithms, and data. It doesn't just replicate the system statically—it simulates, analyzes, predicts, and evolves in response to real-time data from the physical world. In a sense, it transforms raw data into actionable intelligence.

In electrical engineering, where system reliability, efficiency, and safety are paramount, the digital model empowers engineers to visualize system behavior, anticipate failures, test scenarios, and optimize performance—without interrupting actual operations.

Types of Digital Models

a. Physics-Based Models

Physics-based models are developed using the fundamental laws of physics and electrical engineering. These models are deterministic, meaning they rely on well-established equations and relationships.

Examples include:

- Ohm's Law ($V = IR$) to model voltage-current relationships
- Kirchhoff's Laws for current and voltage in circuits
- Thermodynamic equations for heat dissipation in transformers
- Electromagnetic field equations for motor design
- Load flow analysis in power distribution systems

These models are widely used in:

- Circuit simulators like SPICE
- Grid simulation software such as ETAP, PSS/E, or DIgSILENT PowerFactory

Advantages:

- Transparent and explainable behavior
- Grounded in physical principles

- Effective in design-stage modeling and control logic testing

Limitations:

- Often simplified; real-world systems may deviate
- Cannot capture every unpredictable or nonlinear behavior
- Need accurate input parameters, which may change over time

b. Data-Driven Models

Data-driven models use machine learning, deep learning, and statistical algorithms to learn the behavior of the system from historical and real-time data. Rather than relying on predefined equations, these models find patterns and correlations from raw sensor data.

Applications include:

- Predictive maintenance: Forecasting equipment failure based on historical trends
- Fault classification: Identifying and categorizing faults in circuits
- Load forecasting: Predicting electrical demand at different times or seasons
- Energy efficiency optimization using consumption patterns

Algorithms commonly used:

- Neural networks
- Decision trees and random forests
- Support Vector Machines (SVM)
- Time-series forecasting models (ARIMA, LSTM)
- Reinforcement learning for adaptive control

Advantages:

- Adaptive to changing system behavior

- Can model complex, nonlinear interactions
- Useful when physics-based modeling is infeasible

Limitations:

- Black-box behavior: Harder to interpret
- Data quality and volume are critical
- Require constant retraining for accuracy

c. Hybrid Models

Hybrid models combine physics-based and data-driven approaches to get the best of both worlds. These are especially useful in electrical systems where theoretical models exist, but variability and uncertainty require learning from real data.

Use cases:

- A transformer model using physics for core losses and data-driven estimation for oil degradation
- A microgrid model where power flow is based on electrical laws, but load behavior is learned from data

Benefits:

- Higher accuracy and robustness
- Better generalization under varying conditions
- Faster learning and convergence

Hybrid modeling is becoming increasingly popular in Industry 4.0 settings, where systems are complex, interconnected, and data-rich.

Functions of the Digital Model

The digital model goes far beyond static representation. Its main functions include:

1. Visualization

It offers a visual interface—either 2D dashboards or 3D digital replicas—that helps engineers, operators, and managers interact with and monitor the system.

- SCADA-like dashboards for control rooms
- 3D models showing real-time operational data
- Augmented Reality (AR) overlays for field technicians
- Geographical Information Systems (GIS) for power networks

2. Simulation
The model allows for safe and cost-effective experimentation:

- Simulate load changes
- Test fault responses
- Analyze behavior under different environmental conditions
- Study energy consumption under varied usage

Simulation helps in design validation, training, and emergency preparedness.
3. Diagnosis
By continuously comparing the physical system's behavior with expected norms, the digital model identifies:

- Faults or anomalies
- Inefficiencies (e.g., harmonic distortion, power factor issues)
- Degradations in system performance This proactive diagnosis prevents downtime and improves safety.

4. Optimization
Based on real-time data and predictive analytics, the model can recommend or implement:

- Load balancing in power systems
- Optimal operating parameters for motors and drives
- Energy-saving configurations in smart homes or industries

Optimization also supports economic and environmental goals, like reducing operational costs and carbon footprints.

5. Control

The digital model can actively participate in control loops, especially in automated and smart systems:

- Adjusting setpoints for voltage regulators
- Changing operating schedules of distributed energy resources
- Controlling capacitor banks or reactive power compensators

With real-time data, the model ensures feedback-based control that enhances stability and responsiveness.

Continuous Learning and Self-Improvement

A hallmark of a well-designed digital model is its ability to evolve over time. As it ingests more data from the physical system, it becomes smarter and more accurate. This continuous learning loop involves:

- Retraining ML models periodically
- Updating physics models as equipment wears or conditions change
- Integrating new sensors or parameters into the modeling pipeline

This adaptability ensures that the Digital Twin remains relevant and useful throughout the asset's lifecycle—from commissioning to decommissioning.

The Digital Model is the intelligence engine of the Digital Twin. By combining physics, data science, and visualization technologies, it brings systems to life digitally. In the world of electrical engineering, where systems are complex, dynamic, and safety-critical, the digital model enables engineers to understand deeply, act intelligently, and innovate rapidly. As technology advances, these models will become even more immersive, predictive, and autonomous, paving the way for next-generation smart electrical systems.

DATA

In the realm of Digital Twin technology, data is the lifeblood that flows between the physical system and the digital model. It enables synchronization, intelligence, real-time insights, and decision-making capabilities that lie at the heart of a Digital Twin. Without data, even the most sophisticated digital model is blind and ineffective. With accurate, timely, and well-structured data, the Digital Twin becomes a powerful tool for prediction, control, and optimization in electrical engineering applications.

Types of Data in a Digital Twin System

The Digital Twin ecosystem integrates multiple forms of data, each serving specific purposes. These can be broadly classified into the following categories:

Sensor Data

Sensor data is real-time, streaming data collected directly from the physical system. In electrical engineering, this includes:

- Voltage levels across different nodes
- Current measurements on lines or circuits
- Power factor readings
- Frequency deviations
- Harmonic distortion levels
- Temperature of conductors, motors, transformers, etc.
- Vibration and pressure data in electromechanical systems

This data allows the Digital Twin to mirror the current state of the system precisely and enables immediate diagnostics or alerts in case of anomalies.

Operational Data

Operational data provides information about how the system or equipment is functioning over time. It includes:

- Device status (ON/OFF, standby, faulted)
- Usage cycles or run-time statistics

- Control commands and actuator states
- Switching patterns and relay statuses
- System configuration parameters

This type of data helps in understanding system behavior, energy consumption patterns, and performance trends over extended periods.

Historical Data

Historical data captures the past performance and maintenance records of a system or component. It includes:

- Maintenance schedules and logs
- Failure events and root cause analysis
- Downtime history and MTTR (Mean Time to Repair)
- Repair or replacement timelines
- Aging and wear patterns of components

Historical data is essential for predictive maintenance and lifecycle analysis. It helps the Digital Twin recognize trends and anticipate future failures or maintenance needs.

Environmental Data

Environmental conditions have a significant impact on the performance and longevity of electrical systems. Environmental data includes:

- Ambient temperature and humidity
- Wind speed (for wind turbines)
- Solar irradiance (for PV systems)
- Load profiles or grid demand
- Pollution levels or corrosive atmosphere in industrial setups

Including environmental data makes the Digital Twin more realistic and accurate in simulating conditions and predicting system behavior under varying scenarios.

Design and Configuration Data

This is the static data used to build the original digital model. It includes:

- CAD designs and 3D representations of equipment
- Electrical schematics and wiring diagrams
- Equipment specifications (voltage rating, capacity, insulation class)
- Installation parameters and locations
- Manufacturer-provided data sheets

This foundational data provides structural integrity and context to the real-time data, ensuring that the digital replica mirrors the physical design accurately.

The Data Lifecycle in a Digital Twin

To enable the synchronization between physical and digital systems, data passes through several key stages in its lifecycle:

Data Collection

This is the initial step where sensors and IoT-enabled devices embedded in the physical system capture and log relevant parameters. Key considerations at this stage include:

- Sensor precision and sampling rate
- Sensor calibration
- Data granularity (per second, per minute, event-driven)

Modern systems often use edge computing devices (like Raspberry Pi, industrial gateways) to locally pre-process data before transmission.

Data Transmission

Collected data must be transmitted securely and reliably to the digital twin platform. Common communication protocols include:

- MQTT (Message Queuing Telemetry Transport): Lightweight, efficient, and widely used in IoT.

- OPC-UA (Open Platform Communications – Unified Architecture): Industrial-grade, secure, and vendor-neutral.
- IEC 61850: Specific to electrical substation automation.
- Wireless mesh networks, 5G, Ethernet, or fiber links for varying latency and bandwidth needs.

Security and latency are crucial here—real-time control applications demand low latency, whereas monitoring systems tolerate higher delays.

Data Storage

Depending on the application, data may be stored:

- Locally (on edge devices) for quick access and offline scenarios.
- On-premise servers in industrial settings with high security needs.
- Cloud-based platforms (like Azure, AWS, or Google Cloud) for scalability and global access.

Storage considerations include:

- Time-series databases (e.g., InfluxDB, TimescaleDB) for sensor data
- Relational databases for structured, tabular data
- Data lakes for unstructured or semi-structured data

Data Processing

Once stored, data is processed to derive insights using:

- Data analytics pipelines
- Artificial Intelligence (AI) and Machine Learning (ML) models
- Statistical analysis and trend detection algorithms
- Event correlation engines

Processing transforms raw data into meaningful outputs:

- Predictive alerts
- Performance KPIs
- Energy efficiency indices
- Maintenance recommendations

Data Visualization

Processed data is visualized through:

- Dashboards for operational monitoring (e.g., Grafana, Power BI)
- SCADA interfaces for control room environments
- 3D digital twin visualizations
- Augmented Reality (AR) / Virtual Reality (VR) overlays for immersive analysis

Effective visualization ensures that engineers and decision-makers can understand and act on the data intuitively.

Data Governance and Quality

High-quality data is vital to ensure the reliability and usefulness of the Digital Twin. Data-related issues can lead to:

- Model inaccuracies
- False predictions or alarms
- Ineffective control actions
- Regulatory non-compliance

To mitigate this, organizations implement data governance strategies that focus on:

- Data integrity: Ensuring data is accurate and free from corruption.
- Data consistency: Keeping data formats and units uniform.
- Data completeness: Avoiding missing or incomplete records.
- Data security: Using encryption, role-based access, and secure APIs.

- Data provenance: Tracking data origin and transformations for traceability.

In a Digital Twin, data is not just an enabler—it is the engine that drives every insight, decision, and action. From real-time measurements to long-term historical records, from environmental conditions to design blueprints, data forms the basis for a living, breathing, evolving digital counterpart of the physical system. In the context of electrical engineering, where reliability, performance, and safety are critical, robust data infrastructure ensures that the Digital Twin can serve as a trustworthy and intelligent companion to real-world systems. As technology progresses, the volume, variety, and velocity of data will only increase—making data management and governance an even more essential pillar of Digital Twin implementation.

DIGITAL TWIN VS. SIMULATION AND EMULATION

In the evolving landscape of engineering and industrial systems, technologies like Digital Twin, simulation, and emulation have emerged as powerful tools for modeling, analysis, and optimization. However, despite their overlapping characteristics, these terms are not interchangeable. Each serves a unique purpose, operates under different principles, and provides varying degrees of interaction with physical systems. As Digital Twin technology becomes increasingly central to real-time monitoring, predictive maintenance, and system control, it is crucial to distinguish it from traditional simulation and emulation techniques. This section explores the fundamental differences between these approaches, highlighting how Digital Twins extend beyond conventional modeling by establishing a dynamic, data-driven, and bi-directional connection with physical assets. Understanding these distinctions is essential for professionals in electrical engineering to make informed decisions about which tools to use across the system development lifecycle—from design and testing to deployment and operational intelligence.

Fundamental Differences In Purpose And Design

Digital Twin, simulation, and emulation technologies each serve unique purposes and are designed with different objectives and functionalities. While they may share similarities in modeling physical systems, their roles diverge significantly when examined through the lenses of data interaction, system fidelity, and real-world integration.

Digital Twins:

A Digital Twin is a high-fidelity virtual representation of a physical system that is continuously synchronized with its real-world counterpart. Its core purpose is to monitor, analyze, and optimize the physical system throughout its lifecycle, from design and deployment to operation and maintenance.

The architecture of a Digital Twin incorporates:

- Real-time data acquisition from physical assets via IoT sensors
- Cloud and edge computing for data processing and storage
- Machine learning and AI algorithms for analytics and predictive modeling
- Control mechanisms that can influence the physical system based on insights

The bi-directional data flow is the defining feature of a Digital Twin. This means data not only flows from the physical system to the digital model (for monitoring and prediction), but the Digital Twin can also send signals back to the physical system (e.g., to adjust performance settings or trigger maintenance).

For example, in an electrical substation, a Digital Twin can predict transformer aging by analyzing temperature, load, and insulation condition data, then recommend or initiate preventative actions. Thus, Digital Twins are dynamic, living models that evolve with the system they mirror.

Static and Scenario-Based Models

Simulations, by contrast, are isolated and static representations of systems. They are primarily used during the design and analysis phases of engineering projects. Simulations are typically configured with a set of fixed parameters and initial conditions to study how a system behaves under specific scenarios.

Unlike Digital Twins, simulations:

- Do not operate in real-time
- Do not integrate live data feeds
- Are not updated automatically during execution

Their design is focused on understanding hypothetical outcomes. Engineers use simulations to perform "what-if" analyses—such as evaluating power flow under peak load, testing fault tolerance of circuits, or modeling thermal behavior in electrical components.

For instance, in the design of a new electric motor, engineers might simulate various winding configurations to evaluate efficiency and torque characteristics under simulated conditions. However, once the simulation is completed, its model remains unchanged unless manually updated.

Simulations are powerful for optimization and troubleshooting during the pre-deployment stage but lack adaptability during real-world operation.

Emulation:

Emulation serves as a middle ground between simulation and physical implementation. It focuses on replicating the behavior of one system using another—usually in a controlled test environment. Emulators are commonly used to validate software and hardware interactions, especially in embedded systems development.

An emulator mimics how a physical device or system would behave, enabling engineers to:

- Test firmware without the actual hardware
- Observe timing and signal responses
- Debug control logic in real-time-like scenarios

However, emulation has limited environmental awareness. It does not continuously adapt to live data from physical equipment as a Digital Twin does. While it may provide real-time-like interaction, it's often confined to lab setups or development kits and lacks true system integration.

For example, in power electronics, engineers might use a Hardware-in-the-Loop (HIL) emulator to test a digital controller for an inverter. The emulator replicates the inverter's electrical behavior, allowing validation before deployment. Yet, once deployed, this emulator no longer updates or interacts with the physical inverter system—it was a one-time test.

Real-time data integration and feedback mechanisms

One of the most transformative capabilities of Digital Twin (DT) technology is its ability to integrate real-time data from physical systems and translate that data into actionable insights. This live data integration is achieved through a network of sensors, actuators, and IoT (Internet of Things) devices that continuously monitor the operational state of physical assets, environments, or systems. In the realm of electrical engineering, this functionality plays a crucial role, enabling engineers and operators to monitor, predict, and control systems with high precision and responsiveness.

Real-Time Data Acquisition

Digital Twins utilize a continuous data stream from physical devices, such as voltage sensors, current transformers, temperature probes, and circuit status indicators. These sensors are embedded throughout electrical infrastructure—ranging from power plants to substations and smart grids. The collected data may include parameters such as voltage levels, frequency, load demand, power factor, energy losses, and even environmental conditions like humidity and temperature.

This real-time data is transmitted to the Digital Twin platform, often using communication protocols such as MQTT, OPC UA, or Modbus, ensuring that the virtual replica stays synchronized with its physical counterpart. The data is then processed and visualized in dashboards, enabling stakeholders to track performance metrics in real time.

Dynamic Feedback and Adaptive Control

Unlike traditional models or simulations that operate in a closed-loop offline environment, Digital Twins use real-time feedback mechanisms to dynamically adjust system behavior. For example, in a power distribution network, a sudden spike in demand can trigger the Digital Twin to instruct automated systems to reroute power, engage backup generators, or manage load shedding intelligently. These decisions are often supported by embedded machine learning models or rule-based control algorithms that analyze patterns and optimize responses in real time.

This capability is essential in preventing faults, reducing downtimes, and maintaining operational efficiency. Additionally, real-time feedback allows for predictive maintenance, wherein the Digital Twin can foresee potential equipment failures based on vibration patterns, thermal signatures, or historical performance trends, and issue alerts before a breakdown occurs.

Comparison with Simulations and Emulators

- Simulations are valuable for analyzing electrical systems under predefined conditions. They are often used in design and planning stages—for instance, running load flow analysis, fault studies, or harmonic analysis. However, these are static by nature. Simulations do not receive continuous data from the field and cannot adapt in real time. Once the simulation ends, it provides a snapshot, not a living model.

- Emulators are more dynamic than simulations and can mimic real-time conditions. They are widely used in hardware-in-the-loop (HIL) or software-in-the-loop (SIL) environments, particularly in laboratories or testing setups. However, emulators typically simulate signal behaviors rather than monitor and react to actual physical hardware continuously deployed in the field. Their use is limited to developmental or prototyping scenarios.

Why Real-Time Feedback Is Foundational to Digital Twins

The ability to both ingest live data and respond adaptively sets Digital Twins apart. They are not just passive replicas but active systems that evolve with their physical counterparts. This enables engineers to:

- Implement real-time optimization of power systems
- Detect and isolate faults before they escalate
- Ensure energy efficiency through continuous monitoring
- Enable remote diagnostics and control
- Improve decision-making through up-to-date data analytics

In summary, real-time data integration and feedback mechanisms are not just features of the Digital Twin framework—they are its defining pillars. They bridge the gap between static modeling and dynamic operation, allowing electrical systems to become smarter, more resilient, and future-ready.

Application Areas In Electrical Engineering

Digital Twins, simulations, and emulations each play a distinct role in the electrical engineering ecosystem. While they may overlap in function, their applications are typically aligned with different stages of the engineering lifecycle—from design and testing to deployment and maintenance. This section explores where each approach fits in practical, real-world electrical engineering domains, and illustrates their value with specific examples.

Real-Time Operation and Predictive Maintenance

Digital Twins are increasingly being deployed in live, operational environments where ongoing monitoring, diagnostics, and adaptive control are essential. In electrical engineering, this includes:

- Smart Grids: Digital Twins enable real-time monitoring of grid performance, load balancing, and fault localization. They use live sensor data to predict outages, optimize load distribution, and reduce energy losses.

- Substations and Transformers: By continuously analyzing thermal conditions, oil quality, and vibration levels, a Digital Twin can detect anomalies in transformer health and recommend maintenance before a failure occurs.
- Renewable Energy Systems: In wind and solar farms, Digital Twins track performance metrics like rotor speed, energy yield, and inverter efficiency to fine-tune energy output and anticipate equipment degradation.

Example:

1. Digital Twin of a Wind Turbine System

A wind turbine's Digital Twin monitors blade rotation, wind speed, temperature, and vibration data. By feeding this into predictive analytics, operators can schedule blade inspections before critical damage occurs, thus reducing downtime and extending turbine life.

Design, Analysis, and Theoretical Exploration

Simulation tools are indispensable during the planning and design phases of electrical systems. Engineers rely on simulations to validate system behavior under theoretical or expected conditions before building physical prototypes.

Common applications include:

- Power Flow Studies: Simulating how power is distributed across a network to ensure efficient load management and system stability.
- Harmonic Analysis: Studying the impact of nonlinear loads and mitigating issues like voltage distortion or resonance in industrial plants.
- Grounding System Design: Evaluating safety measures in substations by simulating ground fault currents and their dispersion through earth electrodes.

Simulation tools such as MATLAB/Simulink, ETAP, PSpice, and DIgSILENT PowerFactory are frequently used in academia and industry.

Example:

2. Simulation of Harmonic Distortion in an Industrial Network

A simulation of an industrial power distribution system with high-frequency drives helps identify the level of total harmonic distortion (THD). Engineers can then design and test harmonic filters virtually before physical implementation.

Testing and Validation in Real-Time Conditions

Emulation sits between simulation and real-world deployment. It's typically used in hardware-in-the-loop (HIL) and software-in-the-loop (SIL) environments, where physical controllers interact with simulated systems in real time.

Key uses in electrical engineering include:

- Protective Relay Testing: Emulators can mimic fault conditions on a power line, helping engineers test relay response and timing without needing to create actual faults.
- PLC (Programmable Logic Controller) Validation: Control logic written for PLCs can be tested against an emulated process to verify functionality and safety.
- Firmware Development: Embedded systems, such as smart meters or inverter controllers, can be tested with emulated electrical signals before field deployment.

Comparative Advantages And Limitations

To better understand the unique value of each approach in electrical engineering, it's helpful to compare them across key features such as real-time operation, data feedback, application stages, cost, predictive capabilities, and hardware dependency. The following discussion provides insight into the respective strengths of Digital Twins, simulations, and emulations, emphasizing when and why each is most effective.

Digital Twins excel in real-time operation and continuous data feedback, making them particularly valuable during the operational and maintenance phases of an electrical system's lifecycle. Their ability to incorporate live data from sensors, integrate with IoT platforms, and use predictive analytics allows for intelligent decision-making, fault prevention, and optimized performance. However, this capability comes with high infrastructure and implementation costs, as it requires not only software models but also physical integration with real-world hardware and a robust communication network. As such, Digital Twins provide long-term strategic value, especially in complex systems like smart grids, renewable energy farms, or high-voltage substations.

Simulations, on the other hand, are primarily used during the design and planning stages. They do not support real-time operation or continuous feedback but are cost-effective and relatively easy to implement using tools like MATLAB/Simulink, ETAP, or PSpice. Simulations allow engineers to test various theoretical scenarios—such as load flow, fault analysis, or grounding effectiveness—under controlled conditions. While some limited offline predictive analysis is possible, simulations lack the dynamic interactivity and learning capabilities of Digital Twins. Still, they remain indispensable in early-phase development for evaluating design choices and improving system reliability before any hardware is built.

Emulations serve as a bridge between theoretical simulation and real-world deployment. They are especially useful in testing and integration phases, such as firmware validation, protective relay testing, and PLC logic verification. Emulators can simulate electrical behaviors in a lab environment using virtual hardware or testbenches, sometimes in near real-time. They allow engineers to validate device responses to synthetic signals without risking real equipment. However, their feedback capabilities are limited, and they may not be scalable or robust enough for deployment in field conditions. Emulations offer a moderate cost and complexity level, making them ideal for iterative development and hardware-in-the-loop (HIL) testing.

In summary, each approach plays a critical role at different stages of system development and operation. Digital Twins deliver the most comprehensive and future-ready solution but require substantial infrastructure. Simulations are essential for conceptual validation and design prototyping, offering an efficient path for exploring ideas. Emulations are instrumental in testing and debugging, ensuring that systems behave correctly before actual deployment. Understanding these distinctions helps engineers select the right toolset based on project goals, system maturity, and available resources.

FOUR

TYPES OF DIGITAL TWINS

Digital Twin technology is not a one-size-fits-all solution; instead, it spans a spectrum of complexity and functionality based on the specific needs of an engineering environment. As the concept has matured, it has been classified into three primary types—Component Twins, System Twins, and Process Twins—each serving a unique role within the broader context of digital modeling and control. This classification helps engineers, developers, and decision-makers understand how to implement Digital Twins at various levels of abstraction, from the smallest hardware element to a large-scale operational ecosystem.

At the most fundamental level, Component Twins represent individual physical entities such as sensors, actuators, circuit breakers, or transformer coils. These twins mirror the real-time status, performance, and behavior of single components, enabling detailed monitoring and early fault detection at the micro level. For instance, a Component Twin of a high-voltage capacitor might track dielectric breakdown conditions, thermal stress, or voltage fluctuations to predict failure before it occurs. This granular insight is critical in applications where component reliability is paramount and unplanned downtime can have costly repercussions.

Moving beyond individual parts, System Twins provide a virtual representation of an integrated set of components working together as a unit. These systems could range from a power distribution panel to an entire electrical substation. A System Twin not only captures the operational behavior of each internal element but also models the complex interactions between them, such as power flow dynamics, fault propagation, or load balancing logic. These twins enable operators to assess system-level performance, test reconfiguration strategies, and respond dynamically to real-world disturbances, such as voltage dips or phase imbalance.

At the highest level of abstraction, Process Twins model entire workflows or operations involving multiple interconnected systems and processes over time. In electrical engineering, a Process Twin might replicate the sequence of energy production in a power plant, from fuel conversion to grid injection, incorporating aspects such as energy efficiency, environmental controls, and human-machine interactions. These twins are particularly powerful in industrial automation, smart grid coordination, and large-scale infrastructure management, where understanding the end-to-end behavior of a process is essential for optimization, sustainability, and compliance.

Understanding these three types of Digital Twins is critical for engineering professionals aiming to implement digital solutions across the lifecycle of electrical systems. While each type serves a specific purpose, they are not mutually exclusive. In fact, they often function in concert—Component Twins feed data into System Twins, which in turn inform Process Twins. This layered approach creates a scalable and modular framework for real-time monitoring, predictive analytics, and adaptive control. As such, the classification into Component, System, and Process Twins provides a blueprint for digital transformation in electrical engineering, guiding the development of tailored digital strategies that align with both operational goals and technical requirements.

This section delves deeply into each type of Digital Twin, explaining their structure, real-world applications, technological requirements, and benefits. It also highlights how these different types interconnect to form a robust and intelligent digital infrastructure, ultimately enabling more efficient, reliable, and responsive electrical systems.

Digital Twins can be classified based on the scale and complexity of what they represent. The three core categories are Component Twins, System Twins, and Process Twins. Each plays a unique role in modeling, monitoring, and optimizing electrical systems, and together they form a layered approach to digital replication.

Component Twins:

Component Twins are the most granular form of Digital Twins. They represent individual physical parts or devices in a system, such as capacitors, insulators, switches, relays, or sensors. These twins are designed to mirror the behavior, condition, and lifecycle of a single asset.

They continuously collect data on operational metrics like temperature, voltage, current, vibration, or wear and tear, offering engineers detailed insight into the health and performance of that specific component. In electrical systems, even minor component failures can trigger cascading problems—making early detection and predictive maintenance critical.

Applications in Electrical Engineering:

- Monitoring transformer insulation condition
- Tracking switchgear contact wear
- Predicting failure in current sensors or voltage regulators
- Optimizing performance of individual power electronic devices

By focusing on the smallest building blocks, Component Twins help ensure the reliability and safety of the entire system.

System Twins: Replicating Interconnected Electrical Subsystems

System Twins represent a group of components working together as a functional unit. They go beyond individual behavior to model the interactions, dependencies, and dynamics between multiple elements. These twins provide a holistic view of an entire subsystem, such as a distribution board, a solar inverter network, or a substation.

System Twins enable engineers to simulate scenarios, analyze system-level performance, and test different control strategies without disrupting physical operations. They are also vital in implementing smart automation, managing loads, and responding to faults in real time.

Applications in Electrical Engineering:

- Smart substation management and control
- Load flow analysis and automatic reconfiguration
- Integration of renewable sources into grid infrastructure
- System-wide fault detection and response

With System Twins, complex interrelationships between components can be studied and optimized, improving efficiency and resilience.

Process Twins: Capturing Full-Scale Operations and Workflows

Process Twins model entire end-to-end processes, including physical systems, human interactions, and environmental influences. These are the highest-level twins, capable of representing complete operational workflows—such as the energy generation-to-distribution cycle, power plant operations, or industrial electrical automation processes.

They integrate data from multiple System Twins and include logic for process sequencing, timing, resource consumption, and regulatory compliance. These twins are crucial for strategic decision-making, long-term planning, and performance optimization across an entire operation.

Applications in Electrical Engineering:

- Digital replication of a complete smart grid operation
- Energy production process in power plants (thermal, hydro, wind)

- Substation automation with load dispatch coordination
- Optimization of manufacturing processes involving electrical machinery

Process Twins enable insights into systemic bottlenecks, energy inefficiencies, or downtime patterns, guiding improvements across the entire value chain.

Interrelationship and Hierarchical Integration

Although categorized separately, Component, System, and Process Twins do not operate in isolation. In a real-world deployment, these three types are often hierarchically connected:

- Component Twins feed data into System Twins.
- System Twins integrate to form Process Twins.
- Process Twins oversee and coordinate multiple systems and their components.

This layered architecture enables scalable and modular implementation of Digital Twin strategies. It ensures that insights gained at the micro level (e.g., temperature rise in a motor) can inform macro-level decisions (e.g., changing load patterns in a substation or altering maintenance schedules).

Digital Twins rely on a fusion of modern digital technologies to function as real-time, intelligent, and scalable replicas of physical systems. The four core technologies that enable this integration are the Internet of Things (IoT), Artificial Intelligence (AI), Machine Learning (ML), and Cloud Computing. Together, these form the digital backbone of every advanced Digital Twin ecosystem.

Internet of things (IOT)

The Internet of Things (IoT) serves as the foundational layer in the Digital Twin architecture, acting as the sensory and communication system that connects the physical and digital worlds. Without IoT, a Digital Twin would lack the real-time, ground-level data needed to reflect the dynamic state of physical assets. This network of interconnected sensors, actuators, edge devices, and embedded systems is what enables the digital model to stay in sync with its physical counterpart, update in real time, and respond to real-world events and conditions.

IoT as the Sensory Layer

At its core, IoT introduces the ability to *see*, *hear*, and *feel* what's happening in physical systems. In the context of electrical engineering, IoT devices are strategically deployed in field equipment such as:

- **Power transformers** to monitor oil temperature, gas formation, and insulation health
- **Circuit breakers** to detect tripping events, arcing conditions, and contact wear
- **Protective relays** to log fault currents and voltage sag events
- **Solar panels** to track irradiance, panel temperature, and DC output
- **Smart meters** in households and industries for energy usage monitoring

These devices continuously capture multi-dimensional data such as voltage, current, temperature, humidity, frequency variations, load fluctuations, and system health indicators. This stream of sensor data is typically timestamped, geo-tagged, and sent via communication protocols like MQTT, OPC UA, or Modbus to cloud platforms or edge servers for further processing.

Secure and Reliable Data Transmission

A critical function of IoT in the Digital Twin framework is to transmit collected data securely and reliably. Electrical systems, especially in utility environments, operate under stringent cybersecurity requirements. Therefore, the IoT communication layer is designed to handle:

- Secure transmission protocols (e.g., TLS, HTTPS, VPN tunneling)
- Low latency and high-frequency updates for real-time monitoring

- Edge-to-cloud communication pipelines for scalable deployment
- Data filtering and compression to optimize bandwidth and reduce noise

By enabling this seamless data flow, IoT ensures that the Digital Twin receives the most up-to-date information, maintaining digital fidelity to the real asset.

Applications of IoT in Electrical Digital Twins

IoT technology is the key enabler behind many advanced Digital Twin functionalities. Below are some of the most impactful areas:

1. **Real-Time Data Acquisition and Streaming**

IoT allows engineers to monitor equipment status and environmental variables in real time. For instance, in a substation, sensors can instantly detect abnormal temperature rises or vibration patterns in a transformer and update the Digital Twin to reflect these changes, triggering alerts or simulations for corrective action.

1. **Remote Monitoring and Diagnostics**

With IoT-connected Digital Twins, operators can remotely access and monitor assets from control centers or mobile devices. This is particularly valuable for remote or hazardous environments like offshore wind farms or high-voltage substations, reducing the need for physical inspections.

3. **Early Fault Detection and Alerts**

Advanced IoT devices equipped with diagnostic capabilities can detect subtle changes in performance long before a failure occurs. For example, increasing partial discharge levels in a switchgear compartment might indicate insulation breakdown. The Digital Twin, fed with this data, can simulate fault progression and alert maintenance teams.

4. Predictive Maintenance Strategies

IoT-driven data enables the transition from traditional time-based maintenance to condition-based and predictive maintenance. Rather than relying on fixed schedules, Digital Twins can analyze live data trends to predict when equipment is likely to fail, allowing for timely intervention and resource optimization.

IoT as the Physical-Digital Bridge

Ultimately, IoT serves as the digital nervous system of the Digital Twin. It ensures continuous synchronization between the physical asset and its virtual replica by:

- Feeding live operational data to the twin
- Enabling two-way communication for actuation or remote commands
- Creating a closed feedback loop that supports autonomous decision-making

This capability is especially vital in mission-critical electrical systems, such as smart grids, renewable energy farms, and industrial control systems, where real-time insight and rapid response are essential for maintaining stability, safety, and efficiency.

Artificial Intelligence (AI)

Artificial Intelligence (AI) plays a pivotal role in transforming a Digital Twin from a passive data visualization tool into a proactive, decision-making system. It serves as the cognitive engine that interprets vast volumes of real-time data, identifies meaningful insights, and enables intelligent actions. In the context of electrical engineering, where systems are becoming increasingly complex and dynamic, AI is not just an add-on—it is an enabler of automation, efficiency, and resilience.

From Data to Decisions

The foundation of a Digital Twin lies in its ability to replicate a physical asset or system in a digital space using data collected through IoT sensors and embedded systems. However, raw data alone has limited value. This is where AI steps in. AI algorithms—ranging from simple decision trees to advanced deep learning models—are used to process, filter, and analyze incoming data streams.

Through machine learning (ML), the system can learn from historical data, recognize patterns, and make predictions about future states. This allows the Digital Twin to evolve beyond mere mirroring to becoming a foresight-driven platform capable of making informed decisions in real time.

Key Applications of AI in Electrical Engineering Digital Twins

1. Fault Prediction and Root Cause Analysis

AI can anticipate equipment failures or system faults before they occur by analyzing patterns in historical and real-time sensor data. For example:

- Machine learning models trained on voltage fluctuations and temperature variations can predict transformer degradation.
- AI can distinguish between transient and permanent faults, assisting in targeted diagnostics.

Root cause analysis is enhanced through AI-driven correlation analysis. Instead of manually examining vast logs or waveform data, AI can isolate anomalies and trace them back to their origin within the system, reducing downtime and improving system reliability.

2. Decision Automation

AI enables the automation of complex operational decisions such as:

- Switching operations: Identifying and executing optimal switching sequences during contingencies.

- Isolation and re-routing: In the event of a line fault, AI can determine the safest and most efficient re-routing strategy to maintain service continuity.
- Load balancing: Automatically adjusting control mechanisms to ensure equitable distribution of load across substations or feeders.

These intelligent decisions can be made with minimal or no human intervention, which is crucial in high-speed, critical systems such as power grids.

3. Optimization of Grid Performance and Resource Usage

AI-driven optimization algorithms are employed to enhance the efficiency of grid operations. These include:

- Economic dispatch to minimize the cost of power generation.
- Reactive power compensation to maintain voltage levels within acceptable limits.
- Demand forecasting to align power generation with predicted consumption patterns.

By continuously learning and adapting to new operating conditions, AI models ensure that resources are allocated optimally, reducing energy wastage and operational costs.

4. Natural Language Interaction for Maintenance Support

Integrating Natural Language Processing (NLP) with Digital Twins enables intuitive human-machine interaction. Maintenance personnel can query the system in plain language, for example:

- "What is the cause of the voltage drop in Zone 4?"
- "Show me the maintenance history of transformer T5."

AI interprets these queries and retrieves relevant information, making system diagnostics more accessible and less dependent on technical expertise. This improves productivity and supports informed decision-making in the field.

Transforming the Role of Digital Twins

AI transforms a Digital Twin from a static representation into a dynamic, interactive system. With AI, the Digital Twin does not simply report what is happening—it provides insights into why it is happening and what should be done about it.

In the fast-evolving domain of electrical engineering, this capability is vital. Grids are transitioning to include decentralized generation sources, variable loads, and renewable integration. AI-powered Digital Twins provide the necessary intelligence to adapt, optimize, and operate efficiently in such environments.

Ultimately, the fusion of AI and Digital Twins enables:

- Proactive system management
- Reduced operational risk
- Data-driven maintenance planning
- Enhanced decision support for engineers and operators

Machine Learning (ML)

Machine Learning (ML) is a subset of AI that enables the Digital Twin to learn from historical and real-time data. ML models can be trained using past equipment performance, failure logs, environmental factors, and user interactions. Over time, these models improve their accuracy and prediction capability.

In the electrical domain, ML is crucial for applications like load forecasting, energy consumption modeling, predictive maintenance, and anomaly detection. For example, an ML-powered Digital Twin of a power transformer can predict insulation failure months in advance by analyzing historical oil temperature and partial discharge data.

Key Functions of ML in Digital Twins:

- Pattern recognition in sensor data streams
- Predictive analytics for fault and maintenance
- Adaptive control strategies based on system behavior
- Continuous improvement of model accuracy

ML allows Digital Twins to evolve from static replicas to dynamic, learning entities that improve with experience.

Cloud Computing

Cloud Computing offers the digital infrastructure required to deploy, manage, and scale Digital Twin solutions. The massive volume of real-time data collected by IoT devices needs robust processing power, secure storage, and high-speed connectivity — all of which are facilitated by cloud platforms.

With cloud computing, Digital Twins are no longer confined to local systems. They can be deployed across multiple regions, integrated with third-party services, and accessed remotely via dashboards or mobile apps. Cloud platforms also support hybrid models, combining on-premises data with remote analytics.

Key Contributions of Cloud Computing:

- Scalable data storage and high-performance computing
- Real-time communication between physical and digital layers
- Integration with advanced analytics and visualization tools
- Remote access and collaboration for engineering teams

Major cloud providers like Microsoft Azure, AWS, and Google Cloud offer specialized services tailored for Digital Twin development, including simulation environments, AI model training, and secure data pipelines.

Convergence of Technologies

The true power of Digital Twins lies not in individual technologies, but in the seamless convergence of multiple advanced systems—namely, the Internet of Things (IoT), Artificial Intelligence (AI), Machine Learning (ML), and cloud computing. Each of these plays a critical role: IoT acts as the sensory layer, continuously collecting real-time data from electrical systems such as transformers, circuit breakers, and smart meters. AI serves as the decision-making core, interpreting this data to detect anomalies, optimize operations, and enable autonomous control actions. ML enhances this capability by learning from historical and live data, gradually improving the accuracy of predictions, fault detection, and system behavior modeling. Cloud computing, meanwhile, provides the scalable and accessible infrastructure necessary to process, store, and share massive volumes of data across various devices and platforms. When integrated, these technologies create a dynamic feedback-driven ecosystem, where data is continuously collected, analyzed, acted upon, and used for future learning. This convergence transforms Digital Twins from static 3D representations or isolated simulations into living digital entities—capable of real-time monitoring, predictive maintenance, autonomous control, and lifecycle management. Such a unified digital framework is especially vital in electrical engineering, where systems are complex, distributed, and demand high reliability. The result is a smarter, more resilient infrastructure that evolves over time, mirroring the growing complexity and intelligence of modern electrical networks.

FIVE

DIGITAL TWIN ARCHITECTURE

The Digital Twin has emerged as a transformative paradigm in the era of Industry 4.0 and smart infrastructure, offering a powerful way to visualize, monitor, simulate, and optimize physical systems in a digital environment. At the heart of this transformation lies the Digital Twin Architecture—a comprehensive, multilayered framework that defines how data, technology, and intelligence converge to create a functional and responsive digital replica of a real-world asset or system. This architecture is not merely a technical arrangement of components but a strategic foundation that governs how a Digital Twin behaves, evolves, and delivers value across the entire lifecycle of a system. In electrical engineering, where systems are inherently complex, distributed, and mission-critical, the role of architecture becomes even more vital. From substations and transmission lines to smart meters and microgrids, every element in the electrical infrastructure can be modeled, analyzed, and controlled through a well-structured digital twin—enabled by a robust underlying architecture.

Digital Twin Architecture encapsulates several key components, each performing a specific role in ensuring accurate representation and effective operation. These include physical asset connectivity, data acquisition through IoT sensors, data processing and fusion layers, intelligent decision-making via AI/ML models, communication interfaces, visualization dashboards, and integrated control mechanisms. The architecture also defines how these components interact—through data pipelines, APIs, communication protocols (such as MQTT, OPC UA, and RESTful services), and cloud or edge computing infrastructures. It ensures that real-time data captured from the physical environment is securely transmitted, processed, and made actionable in a digital format. Moreover, the architecture accounts for historical data storage, data synchronization, cybersecurity protocols, and system scalability—making it resilient, adaptive, and future-ready.

A distinguishing feature of Digital Twin Architecture is its modularity and layered design. Typically, it is composed of several interoperable layers, each focusing on a specific function. The Perception Layer deals with sensor integration and real-time data acquisition. The Network Layer manages data transmission and communication infrastructure. The Data Layer is responsible for aggregation, cleansing, and storage of data. The Modeling and Simulation Layer focuses on generating accurate digital representations and running simulations for predictive analysis. The Intelligence Layer incorporates AI and ML algorithms for diagnostics, optimization, and decision-making. Finally, the Application Layer presents the processed insights to users through dashboards, alerts, and control interfaces. This multi-tiered structure allows for high flexibility, where each layer can be upgraded or replaced without affecting the rest of the system, supporting long-term sustainability and adaptability.

In addition to technical elements, the architecture also emphasizes interoperability and integration with legacy systems. In real-world electrical networks, various devices and platforms—many of which have been in use for decades—must be included in the digital transformation process. The architecture must support hybrid environments, where modern smart devices coexist with older analog equipment. Through protocol converters, data adapters, and middleware layers, a well-designed architecture ensures seamless integration, allowing the Digital Twin to offer a unified view of the entire electrical ecosystem. This capability is essential for utilities and industries aiming to modernize their operations without undergoing complete infrastructure overhauls.

Furthermore, scalability and deployment strategy are central considerations within the architectural design. Depending on the complexity and scope of the application, Digital Twins can be deployed at different scales—from a single asset (e.g., a transformer or circuit breaker) to an entire facility or network (e.g., a power distribution system or smart city grid). The architecture must therefore be capable of supporting edge computing for latency-sensitive applications, cloud computing for centralized analytics, or a hybrid model that balances both. This flexibility is critical in addressing diverse use cases such as real-time monitoring, energy management, fault diagnostics, operational planning, and strategic forecasting in electrical systems.

Another essential dimension of Digital Twin Architecture is security and governance. Since Digital Twins rely heavily on continuous data exchange between the physical and digital domains, they are exposed to cybersecurity risks. The architecture must include robust security mechanisms such as encryption, authentication, authorization, and anomaly detection. It should also comply with industry standards and data governance policies to ensure privacy, data integrity, and compliance with regulatory frameworks. Additionally, role-based access control, audit trails, and secure APIs form integral parts of the architecture to safeguard both operational and strategic digital assets.

From a lifecycle perspective, Digital Twin Architecture supports not just operational efficiency but also long-term asset management. It enables a shift from reactive to predictive and ultimately prescriptive maintenance. Engineers can simulate system responses to various conditions, plan upgrades or replacements, and assess the impact of design changes without physical intervention. This proactive capability results in reduced downtime, optimized resource allocation, and extended asset lifespan—key objectives in the electrical engineering domain, where reliability and availability are paramount.

In essence, Digital Twin Architecture acts as the central nervous system of the entire digital twin ecosystem. It brings together sensing technologies, computational intelligence, communication protocols, and human interfaces into a coherent, responsive structure. The architectural design determines how well the digital twin performs under different scenarios—how fast it responds, how accurately it predicts, how securely it operates, and how easily it integrates with existing systems. As the field of electrical engineering continues to evolve toward greater automation, decentralization, and sustainability, a robust and forward-thinking digital twin architecture becomes not just a technical necessity, but a strategic enabler of innovation and resilience.

This section will delve deeper into the structural layers of Digital Twin Architecture, explain each component's role and function, explore best practices in design and deployment, and examine real-world examples of architectural implementation in electrical engineering contexts. By understanding the architectural underpinnings, engineers, system integrators, and decision-makers can harness the full potential of Digital Twins—not just as a tool for monitoring assets, but as a powerful platform for intelligent, data-driven system evolution.

FRAMEWORK OVERVIEW

A Digital Twin is not a single technology or component, but a comprehensive ecosystem built upon an integrated framework. This framework serves as the architectural foundation that orchestrates the interaction between the physical and digital worlds. It defines how different technologies, data sources, processing systems, and decision-making tools come together to form a cohesive, intelligent system. In electrical engineering, where real-time performance, safety, and reliability are non-negotiable, this framework ensures that every part of the Digital Twin—from sensing to actuation—works seamlessly and efficiently.

The Digital Twin Framework can be visualized as a layered model, where each layer has specific responsibilities but works in harmony with the others to deliver real-time simulation, control, and optimization. This modular and scalable structure enables the Digital Twin to adapt to a wide range of electrical systems, from individual devices like transformers or motors, to large-scale systems such as substations, grids, or smart cities. The core idea of the framework is to ensure continuous synchronization between the physical asset and its digital counterpart, allowing accurate monitoring, predictive analysis, and intelligent intervention.

At its foundation, the framework begins with the Physical Layer, which comprises the real-world electrical components and systems—power lines, substations, circuit breakers, generators, etc. These assets are equipped with IoT-enabled sensors and actuators that continuously collect operational data such as voltage, current, temperature, pressure, and frequency. This layer bridges the physical world with the digital world and serves as the first step in the data pipeline.

Next is the Data Acquisition and Communication Layer, which handles the secure transmission of data from field devices to centralized or edge-based processing units. This layer uses communication protocols such as MQTT, OPC UA, Modbus, or DNP3 to transmit data efficiently and reliably. It ensures data integrity, low latency, and proper time-stamping, which are critical for real-time performance and accurate modeling. Gateways and edge computing devices may be used at this stage to perform local preprocessing and filtering of data before sending it to higher layers.

The Data Management Layer follows, responsible for storing, organizing, and cleansing data collected from various sources. In electrical engineering, where data is produced at high volume and velocity, this layer often employs cloud-based databases or hybrid storage systems that can handle structured and unstructured data. It supports historical data archiving for trend analysis and machine learning, while also maintaining real-time data streams for current operations.

Above this is the Modeling and Simulation Layer, where the core of the Digital Twin resides. Here, digital models of electrical systems are created using simulation tools, CAD models, physics-based models, or data-driven models. These models simulate the behavior of the physical system under different conditions, allowing for virtual testing, system validation, and scenario planning. For example, load flow simulations, fault analysis, and thermal modeling of transformers can be executed in this layer. The models are continuously updated with live data to reflect the current operational status of the physical system.

The Analytics and Intelligence Layer adds intelligence to the Digital Twin framework. This is where AI and Machine Learning algorithms are applied to identify anomalies, predict failures, optimize energy usage, and support autonomous decision-making. It enables advanced functions such as predictive maintenance, demand forecasting, fault root cause analysis, and real-time optimization. As the system learns from historical patterns and real-time data, its predictive capabilities grow, making it increasingly proactive and self-improving.

The Application and Visualization Layer serves as the human-machine interface. It includes dashboards, mobile apps, control panels, and AR/VR interfaces that allow engineers and operators to interact with the Digital Twin. This layer converts raw data and analytical results into meaningful visualizations—heatmaps, graphs, alerts, and reports—that support informed decision-making. Operators can simulate changes, plan maintenance schedules, or respond to faults directly from these interfaces, enhancing operational efficiency and safety.

Cross-cutting all layers is the Security and Governance Layer, which ensures that the entire framework operates in a secure and compliant manner. In electrical systems, where threats like cyberattacks or data breaches can have catastrophic consequences, this layer implements encryption, access control, authentication, and compliance with industry regulations (such as IEC 61850 or

NERC CIP). It also includes policies for data ownership, privacy, and auditability.

The true strength of the Digital Twin Framework lies in its interoperability and extensibility. It is designed to be vendor-neutral and modular, enabling integration with existing systems (SCADA, EMS, DMS), third-party analytics platforms, and future technologies. It supports plug-and-play capabilities, allowing new devices, models, or applications to be added with minimal disruption.

In summary, the Digital Twin Framework in electrical engineering serves as a robust, layered architecture that harmonizes data collection, processing, modeling, intelligence, and user interaction. It ensures that the Digital Twin not only mirrors the physical asset but also enhances its performance through actionable insights and intelligent control. By providing a structured, scalable, and secure foundation, this framework enables the deployment of Digital Twins at every level of the electrical infrastructure—paving the way for smarter, safer, and more efficient energy systems.

DATA ACQUISITION AND INTEGRATION

Data is the lifeblood of any Digital Twin. Without accurate, timely, and well-structured data, even the most advanced models and algorithms cannot provide reliable results. The Data Acquisition and Integration layer is therefore one of the most critical components of Digital Twin architecture. It serves as the bridge between the physical and digital worlds—responsible for gathering data from real-world electrical assets and ensuring that this data is properly integrated into the digital twin environment for processing, analysis, and decision-making.

Data Acquisition:

Data acquisition begins with the deployment of sensors, smart meters, and edge devices on physical electrical infrastructure. These devices are embedded in systems such as transformers, circuit breakers, switchgear, transmission lines, substations, and distributed energy resources (DERs) like solar panels or wind turbines. The goal is to continuously monitor key operational parameters including:

- Voltage and current
- Frequency
- Power factor
- Load levels
- Temperature
- Vibration
- Oil levels (in transformers)
- Fault status and event logs
- Environmental data (e.g., humidity, wind speed for renewable sources)

These sensors collect both static data (e.g., equipment nameplate data, installation details) and dynamic data (e.g., real-time operational values). In mission-critical systems like power grids, high-speed data acquisition is essential to capture transient events such as surges, faults, or overloads.

Many modern devices also include edge computing capabilities, allowing some preliminary processing—such as filtering, aggregation, or anomaly detection—to occur directly at the source before the data is transmitted.

Communication Infrastructure:

Once data is captured, it must be reliably transmitted from the field to central or distributed digital twin platforms. This is where communication protocols and network infrastructure come into play. In electrical engineering applications, common communication technologies include:

- Wired protocols: Modbus, DNP3, IEC 61850 (used extensively in substations)
- Wireless protocols: ZigBee, LoRaWAN, Wi-Fi, LTE/5G
- Message-oriented middleware: MQTT (lightweight, ideal for IoT), AMQP

- Industrial Ethernet: PROFINET, EtherCAT

To ensure real-time performance, low-latency and high-reliability communication is essential, especially for time-sensitive applications like protection systems and demand-response management. Gateways and protocol converters are often used to standardize and translate data formats from heterogeneous sources into a unified format for the digital twin system.

Integration

The integration phase involves combining data from multiple sources—often using different formats, units, sampling rates, and data structures—into a cohesive, centralized data platform. This is a complex and essential task because digital twins typically rely on multisource, multimodal data to function effectively.

Types of data sources integrated in this stage include:

- Operational Technology (OT) systems: SCADA, EMS (Energy Management Systems), DMS (Distribution Management Systems)
- Information Technology (IT) systems: ERP (Enterprise Resource Planning), Asset Management Systems, GIS (Geographic Information Systems)
- Historical databases: Event logs, maintenance records, and past performance data
- External sources: Weather data, market prices, regulatory data

Integration tools and platforms—such as ETL pipelines (Extract, Transform, Load), data lakes, and real-time streaming services like Apache Kafka—are used to collect, cleanse, normalize, and store this data. During integration, data is often enriched with metadata, tagged with timestamps, assigned geographic coordinates, and aligned with a common data model or ontology to ensure semantic consistency.

This integrated dataset becomes the single source of truth for the Digital Twin, enabling consistent analysis, simulation, and decision-making across the system.

Challenges in Data Acquisition and Integration

While this process is foundational to a functional Digital Twin, it comes with a number of challenges:

- Data silos: In many organizations, valuable data is locked away in isolated systems or legacy devices that do not easily interconnect.
- Inconsistent formats: Electrical systems often use vendor-specific protocols or data models, making harmonization difficult.
- Data quality: Noise, missing values, or incorrect calibration of sensors can compromise data accuracy.
- Latency and bandwidth limitations: Particularly in remote or high-load environments, real-time transmission can be constrained.
- Security and privacy: Data must be protected during transmission and storage to prevent breaches and unauthorized access.

Addressing these challenges requires careful planning, adherence to industry standards (such as CIM—Common Information Model, and IEC 61850), and the use of scalable, flexible integration tools.

Role in the Digital Twin Lifecycle

Data acquisition and integration are not one-time tasks—they are continuous and dynamic processes. As the physical system evolves (e.g., new assets are installed, or old ones are upgraded), the acquisition and integration mechanisms must adapt accordingly. Moreover, the success of higher-level functions like AI analytics, machine learning predictions, and automated control depends heavily on the accuracy, completeness, and freshness of the acquired data.

This layer also supports feedback loops: the digital twin analyzes and learns from the data, sends recommendations or commands back to the physical system, and then receives new data in return—thus creating a closed-loop intelligent system.

The Data Acquisition and Integration layer is the foundation on which the digital twin is built. It captures the real-world behavior of electrical systems through sensors and devices, transmits that data using robust communication protocols, and integrates diverse data streams into a unified, actionable digital ecosystem. In doing so, it enables the higher functions of a digital twin—real-time monitoring, predictive maintenance, fault diagnosis, and intelligent control. For electrical engineering applications, where systems are complex, interconnected, and highly sensitive to failures, this layer plays a pivotal role in ensuring the reliability, intelligence, and responsiveness of digital twin solutions.

COMMUNICATION PROTOCOLS AND STANDARDS

In the rapidly evolving landscape of electrical engineering, Digital Twins are transforming how systems are designed, monitored, maintained, and optimized. However, the true potential of a Digital Twin can only be realized when the communication infrastructure enabling data flow is efficient, reliable, and secure. This is where communication protocols and standards come into play. They act as the language and grammar through which the digital and physical components of a system interact—facilitating the seamless exchange of information across heterogeneous devices, platforms, and environments.

The Role of Communication in Digital Twin Ecosystems

Communication protocols are the foundation that binds various components of the digital twin architecture. From data acquisition at the sensor level to cloud-based analysis and human-machine interactions, every layer of the digital twin relies on structured, timely communication.

In essence, these protocols and standards enable:

- Data collection from field devices (sensors, actuators, meters).
- Real-time data streaming for status updates and event triggers.
- Remote command and control of devices.

- Interoperability between multi-vendor systems.
- Scalability and integration with cloud platforms and AI engines.
- Security in data transmission, preventing unauthorized access or manipulation.

Digital Twins in electrical engineering demand high performance due to the critical nature of power systems. Communication delays or inaccuracies can lead to service disruptions, safety hazards, or equipment damage. Thus, choosing the appropriate protocols and complying with relevant standards is essential for building trustworthy and resilient Digital Twin applications.

Commonly Used Communication Protocols

Digital Twin environments in electrical systems utilize a range of communication protocols, each suited to different parts of the system—field level, edge, control center, and cloud. These protocols vary in complexity, performance, scalability, and security. Below are the most widely used:

a. Modbus (RTU / TCP)

Modbus is one of the oldest and most widely adopted industrial protocols. It operates over serial (RTU) or Ethernet (TCP) lines and is used for simple data exchange between devices like sensors, meters, and PLCs.

- Advantages:

  - Easy to implement.
  - Open and royalty-free.
  - Well-suited for legacy devices.

- Limitations:

  - No encryption or authentication.
  - Limited bandwidth and address space.
  - Better suited for small systems or backward compatibility.

b. DNP3 (Distributed Network Protocol)

DNP3 is heavily used in SCADA systems for utility automation. It supports time-stamped events, buffered reporting, and polling mechanisms.

- Advantages:

  - Efficient for remote systems over unreliable networks.
  - Supports secure authentication extensions (DNP3-SA).

- Limitations:

  - More complex than Modbus.
  - Requires careful configuration to ensure interoperability.

c. IEC 61850

IEC 61850 is a globally recognized standard specifically designed for substation automation systems. It supports real-time control through services like GOOSE (Generic Object-Oriented Substation Event) and Sampled Values.

- Advantages:

  - Fast, event-based messaging for protection.
  - Interoperable data models using logical nodes.
  - Designed for scalability and future-proofing.

- Limitations:

  - Requires specialized knowledge for configuration.
  - Higher initial deployment cost.

d. OPC UA (Unified Architecture)

OPC UA is a platform-independent, service-oriented protocol that supports secure and structured data exchange between devices and applications.

- Advantages:

    ○ Rich information modeling.
    ○ End-to-end security (encryption, authentication).
    ○ Suitable for edge-to-cloud and IT/OT integration.

- Limitations:

    ○ More complex to implement compared to simpler protocols.

e. MQTT (Message Queuing Telemetry Transport)

MQTT is a lightweight publish/subscribe protocol widely used in IoT systems. It's ideal for constrained devices and low-bandwidth environments.

- Advantages:

    ○ Low overhead.
    ○ Supports asynchronous messaging.
    ○ Works well for high-frequency telemetry in Digital Twins.

- Limitations:

    ○ Lacks strong data modeling support natively.
    ○ Security must be implemented separately.

f. REST APIs and WebSockets

These are commonly used for integrating web-based applications, dashboards, mobile apps, and cloud services with Digital Twins.

- Advantages:

- Ubiquitous and easy to integrate.
- Real-time updates using WebSockets.
- Ideal for visualization and user interaction layers.

- Limitations:

  - Requires internet connectivity.
  - Typically used for higher layers of the architecture.

Key Industry Standards

Communication protocols are often accompanied by industry standards that define data models, naming conventions, behavior, and interaction rules. These standards ensure consistency, interoperability, and regulatory compliance.

a. IEC 61850

- Defines not just the protocol but also the data structure and services for substation automation.
- Supports logical nodes that encapsulate common functions (e.g., circuit breaker, voltage transformer).
- Enables interoperability between devices from different manufacturers.

b. IEC 61970 and IEC 61968 (CIM - Common Information Model)

- CIM provides a standardized way to model electrical assets, network topology, and business processes.
- Enables integration between SCADA, EMS, GIS, and asset management tools.
- Crucial for unified data representation across the entire utility enterprise.

c. IEEE 2030.5 (Smart Energy Profile)

- Designed for two-way communication in smart grids.
- Supports communication with DERs (solar inverters, EV chargers).
- Facilitates demand-response, real-time pricing, and grid-balancing operations.

d. ISO/IEC 27001 & NIST Cybersecurity Framework

- While not communication protocols per se, these standards provide guidelines to ensure data integrity, confidentiality, and availability.
- Essential for implementing secure communication in Digital Twin architectures.

Integration and Interoperability

One of the most complex challenges in Digital Twin implementation is integrating devices and systems that use different protocols. This is particularly true in large utilities where older legacy systems coexist with modern IoT-enabled equipment.

Solutions include:

- Protocol gateways: Convert messages from one protocol to another (e.g., Modbus to OPC UA).
- Middleware platforms: Act as brokers for multi-protocol communication.
- Common data models: Use of CIM or semantic mapping tools to unify diverse data structures.

Interoperability ensures that data flows without friction, enabling accurate modeling, prediction, and control in the Digital Twin environment.

Cybersecurity Considerations

Digital Twins, when integrated with external networks, become susceptible to cyber threats. Unsecured communication can lead to data tampering, unauthorized control, or system sabotage.

To mitigate risks:

- Use encrypted protocols (e.g., OPC UA with TLS).
- Implement role-based access control.
- Regularly audit and patch communication modules.
- Segment networks to isolate critical systems from public interfaces.

Adopting secure communication practices and aligning with cybersecurity standards is non-negotiable in critical infrastructure like power systems.

Future Trends in Communication for Digital Twins

As digital twin technologies mature, communication protocols and standards are evolving to meet new demands:

- Time-Sensitive Networking (TSN): Deterministic Ethernet protocols for real-time industrial communication.
- 5G and Beyond: Ultra-reliable low-latency communications (URLLC) to support edge-based digital twins.
- Edge-native protocols: Lightweight, AI-integrated protocols for decentralized processing.
- Digital Twin Interoperability Standards (DTIS): Emerging efforts to standardize how twins communicate with each other across domains.

The success of a Digital Twin in electrical engineering is deeply rooted in its communication backbone. Protocols like IEC 61850, MQTT, OPC UA, and DNP3, combined with industry standards such as CIM and IEEE 2030.5, create a robust and flexible framework for real-time data exchange, control, and intelligence. As systems become more complex and interconnected, the demand for interoperable, scalable, and secure communication frameworks continues to grow. Therefore, understanding and strategically applying these protocols and standards is not just a technical necessity—it is a foundational pillar for realizing the full promise of

Digital Twins in modern electrical systems.

DIGITAL MODELING AND SYSTEM IDENTIFICATION

At the core of every Digital Twin lies a digital model—a high-fidelity virtual representation of a physical system or process. This digital model is not merely a static 3D rendering; it is a dynamic, data-driven construct that captures the behavior, characteristics, and interactions of its real-world counterpart. For the Digital Twin to function accurately, it must reflect both the structural and operational intricacies of the physical system it mirrors. This is where digital modeling and system identification play a pivotal role.

Digital Modeling

Digital modeling is the process of creating a virtual representation of a physical asset, system, or process. In the context of electrical engineering, this could involve modeling components such as transformers, circuit breakers, relays, generators, power lines, or even entire substations and grids.

Digital models can vary in complexity and purpose:

- Geometric models: Focus on physical dimensions, layout, and topology.
- Behavioral models: Simulate system responses to inputs or changing conditions (e.g., load variations).
- Functional models: Represent how subsystems interact to perform specific operations.
- Predictive models: Use data and algorithms to forecast performance, detect faults, or optimize processes.

These models are created using mathematical equations, logical rules, and physical laws (such as Ohm's law, Kirchhoff's rules, etc.). Tools like MATLAB/Simulink, PSCAD, ETAP, and digital design platforms are often used to build and simulate such models.

System Identification

System identification refers to the methodology of building mathematical models of a system using measured data. In contrast to purely theoretical modeling, system identification allows for capturing the real behavior of complex electrical systems where first-principles modeling may be difficult or impractical.

This involves:

- Collecting input-output data from the real system (e.g., voltage in, current out).
- Selecting a model structure (e.g., transfer functions, state-space models).
- Estimating model parameters using algorithms (e.g., least squares, neural networks).
- Validating the model by comparing simulated outputs with actual measurements.

System identification is particularly useful in:

- Nonlinear or time-varying systems where conventional modeling is limited.
- Adaptive Digital Twins that learn and evolve with system changes.
- Predictive maintenance, where real-time data is used to predict equipment degradation.

Types of Models in Electrical Digital Twins

Several types of models are used in digital twin architecture based on the intended function:

a. Physical or Physics-Based Models

- Derived from physical laws and known relationships.
- Used in power flow analysis, fault detection, and stability studies.
- Example: Modeling transformer behavior using equivalent circuit parameters.

b. Data-Driven Models

- Developed using machine learning or statistical analysis.
- Require large datasets for training.
- Used in anomaly detection, load forecasting, or failure prediction.

c. Hybrid Models

- Combine physical principles with data-driven insights.
- Achieve better accuracy and adaptability.
- Common in modern digital twins to handle real-world uncertainties.

Model Fidelity and Granularity

Digital models can vary in **fidelity** (level of detail) and **granularity** (scope and resolution):

- **Low-fidelity models**: Simplified, used for broad system-level simulations.
- **High-fidelity models**: Capture intricate behaviors and interactions, suitable for protection design or optimization tasks.
- **Component-level models**: Focus on individual assets (e.g., a relay or breaker).
- **System-level models**: Represent subsystems like a distribution network or microgrid.

The choice depends on application needs—e.g., real-time grid monitoring may use simplified models for speed, while fault analysis may require high-fidelity detail.

Tools and Techniques for Modeling and Identification

Several platforms and techniques are employed in digital modeling and system identification, such as:

- Simulation Software: PSCAD, MATLAB/Simulink, DIgSILENT PowerFactory.

- SCADA and IoT Data: Used to collect real-time input-output data for identification.
- Frequency Response Analysis: For dynamic modeling of components like inverters or motors.
- Neural Networks and AI Models: For complex nonlinear system modeling and learning from historical data.
- Finite Element Analysis (FEA): For detailed thermal and mechanical simulations of electrical machines.

Challenges in Digital Modeling and System Identification

Creating accurate models is not without difficulties:

- Data Quality: Incomplete, noisy, or inconsistent data affects accuracy.
- Model Complexity: High-fidelity models may be computationally intensive.
- Parameter Estimation: Requires expertise and may need calibration over time.
- System Dynamics: Electrical systems are influenced by external and internal factors (e.g., weather, load types), making them hard to model perfectly.

Overcoming these challenges involves a mix of good sensor infrastructure, robust data acquisition, algorithm tuning, and iterative validation.

Continuous Model Updating

One of the key characteristics of Digital Twins is their ability to evolve. Models are not static; they must be updated as the physical system undergoes changes—due to wear, upgrades, environmental factors, or load variation.

Continuous system identification enables this by:

- Monitoring changes in behavior.
- Automatically tuning model parameters.

- Ensuring the digital twin remains synchronized with its physical counterpart.

This adaptability transforms Digital Twins into living digital replicas—capable of self-adjustment and self-learning.

8. Real-World Applications

In electrical engineering, digital modeling and system identification are applied in various real-world use cases:

- Transformer Health Monitoring: Modeling thermal profiles and estimating insulation aging using operational data.
- Fault Location: Identifying exact fault location by modeling impedance and comparing voltage-current patterns.
- Smart Grid Optimization: Modeling load behavior across a distribution feeder to optimize switching and demand response.
- Generator Modeling: Capturing dynamic behavior under varying loads for frequency regulation and stability control.

Digital modeling and system identification are the foundational elements that bring a Digital Twin to life. By mathematically capturing the behavior of electrical components and systems—either through physical laws or data-driven insights—these methods ensure the digital representation remains relevant, reliable, and robust. In modern power systems where complexity is ever-increasing, the ability to model and adaptively identify system behavior in real-time is invaluable. This forms the backbone of a predictive, intelligent, and self-healing electrical infrastructure—an ultimate goal of Digital Twin implementation.

CYBER-PHYSICAL SYSTEMS (CPS)

A Cyber-Physical System (CPS) represents an integrated framework where computational elements (software and algorithms) interact seamlessly with physical processes (hardware and machinery). These systems are designed to monitor and control the physical world through sensors, actuators, and control units, enabling real-time feedback and interaction between the cyber (computational) and physical worlds. The interactions in CPS are deeply intertwined, where changes in physical conditions can influence computational decisions, and vice versa, creating a closed-loop feedback system that operates in real-time.

In the context of Digital Twins and Electrical Engineering, CPS serves as the foundation for creating intelligent, adaptive, and autonomous systems that continuously interact with their physical counterparts. This integration of real-world dynamics with digital decision-making allows engineers to gain a deep understanding of system behavior, improve performance, and predict future outcomes based on live data.

Cyber-Physical System

A Cyber-Physical System is not just a collection of hardware or software; it is a complex system that fuses physical and digital components. It involves:

- Cyber Elements: These are the digital or computational components that perform data processing, decision-making, and communication. They include embedded systems, controllers, communication networks, and computational algorithms.
- Physical Elements: These are the real-world entities, such as machines, sensors, actuators, and the processes they control. In electrical engineering, these elements can include transformers, generators, grid infrastructure, and energy storage devices.
- Communication Network: An essential aspect of CPS, which allows for the seamless exchange of data between physical components and computational systems. These networks can be wired or wireless and enable real-time control and monitoring.

The interplay between cyber and physical components in a CPS facilitates continuous system behavior monitoring, decision-making, and adjustments based on real-time data.

Key Characteristics of CPS

Cyber-Physical Systems have several distinctive features that make them suitable for modern engineering applications, particularly in domains like electrical grids, manufacturing, and smart cities. These characteristics include:

Real-Time Operation: CPS must process and respond to inputs in real-time, meaning the system must update its state and perform actions without noticeable delays. In electrical grids, for example, real-time data helps control load balancing, fault detection, and power distribution.

Autonomous Operation: Many CPS can operate autonomously by making decisions based on predefined algorithms and real-time data. For instance, an electrical grid's CPS might automatically adjust voltage or reroute power to compensate for faults without human intervention.

Adaptability: CPS systems can learn from historical data, adapt to new conditions, and continuously optimize their performance. Machine learning (ML) and artificial intelligence (AI) models allow CPS to adjust based on changing input conditions, enabling systems to self-correct or improve over time.

Distributed Control: The architecture of CPS is typically distributed, meaning control is spread across multiple systems or devices rather than centralized in one location. In power systems, this means sensors, controllers, and other components in different geographical locations are all interconnected to make holistic decisions.

Interactivity: CPS fosters continuous interaction between the physical and computational aspects of the system. For instance, real-time monitoring of grid assets allows for immediate system adjustments based on current conditions.

Safety and Reliability: Many CPS are deployed in critical infrastructures, such as electrical grids, healthcare, or transportation, where safety and reliability are paramount. These systems must maintain continuous operation, even in the event of component failures or unexpected inputs.

Components of CPS

To fully grasp the workings of a Cyber-Physical System, it is important to understand its core components, which can be grouped into three primary categories: physical systems, cyber systems, and communication networks.

a. Physical Systems (The Real-World Entities)

These are the components that represent the actual physical environment, including machinery, equipment, and devices. In electrical engineering, this could include power generation units, transformers, circuit breakers, and even entire electrical grids.

- Sensors: These are devices that collect data from the physical system. In electrical grids, sensors could measure temperature, voltage, current, and power consumption. Sensors are crucial for providing real-time data on the status of the system, such as detecting faults in equipment or variations in load demand.
- Actuators: Actuators are devices that make physical changes to the system based on commands from the cyber component. For example, in electrical systems, actuators might control the opening and closing of circuit breakers, adjust the position of a transformer tap changer, or regulate the flow of electricity to various parts of the grid.

b. Cyber Systems (Computational Elements)

The cyber components of CPS include the computational devices that process, analyze, and interpret the data received from physical systems. These include:

- Embedded Systems: These are small, dedicated devices that perform specific tasks within a physical system. For example, an embedded system in a transformer could continuously monitor its condition and trigger a shutdown if any dangerous thresholds are exceeded.
- Control Algorithms: These algorithms process the data from sensors to make decisions. In an electrical grid, control algorithms may determine how to reroute power or balance load demand during peak times.

- Computational Models: These models are used to simulate physical processes and predict future system behavior. For example, Digital Twins utilize computational models to simulate the behavior of physical assets and systems, allowing engineers to test different scenarios without impacting the real-world system.

c. Communication Networks

Communication networks are the medium through which the cyber and physical components exchange information. These networks enable real-time data transfer and decision-making. Key communication technologies used in CPS include:

- Wired Networks: These are typically used in industrial settings for high-reliability applications, such as Ethernet, Modbus, or IEC 61850 for energy management in smart grids.
- Wireless Networks: Technologies like Zigbee, LoRaWAN, and Wi-Fi are increasingly used to transmit data from remote sensors or devices. In smart grids, wireless networks enable data collection from geographically dispersed assets.
- Edge Computing: Edge computing plays a crucial role in CPS by enabling localized data processing near the data source, minimizing latency and reducing the need for centralized data storage. This is particularly useful for time-sensitive applications like fault detection and response.

CPS in Electrical Engineering

The integration of Cyber-Physical Systems in electrical engineering has ushered in a new era of smart, interconnected, and intelligent power systems. CPS provides numerous benefits, including enhanced monitoring, automation, fault detection, and predictive maintenance. Some key applications in electrical systems include:

a. Smart Grids

Smart grids are perhaps the most prominent example of CPS in electrical engineering. They integrate advanced communication, computing, and control technologies to optimize electricity distribution, reduce energy consumption, and improve grid reliability.

- Real-time Monitoring: Sensors continuously monitor parameters such as voltage, current, and load in real-time. This data feeds into computational systems that use algorithms to adjust the grid's operations.
- Fault Detection and Isolation: CPS can automatically detect faults in the grid (e.g., short circuits or outages) and take corrective actions, such as isolating affected sections or rerouting power to maintain service.
- Demand Response: CPS allows utilities to adjust energy consumption patterns based on real-time demand, making the grid more efficient. For example, by remotely controlling appliances or charging stations, the grid can flatten peak demand and prevent overloads.

b. Renewable Energy Systems
CPS also plays a vital role in integrating renewable energy sources, such as solar, wind, and hydroelectric power, into the electrical grid.

- Variable Energy Output Management: Solar and wind power generation is often variable and unpredictable. CPS helps manage the integration of these energy sources by constantly monitoring environmental conditions and adjusting grid operations.
- Energy Storage: CPS enables efficient management of energy storage systems, such as batteries, by controlling when to charge and discharge based on grid conditions and renewable energy availability.

c. Predictive Maintenance and Fault Prevention

By using real-time sensor data and predictive algorithms, CPS systems can predict when equipment is likely to fail and schedule maintenance before a breakdown occurs. This approach minimizes downtime and ensures continuous operation of critical infrastructure.

- Health Monitoring: Sensors in equipment like transformers, circuit breakers, and motors monitor key parameters, such as temperature, vibration, and pressure, to assess the health of the system.
- Anomaly Detection: By analyzing trends in sensor data, CPS can detect anomalies early—such as unusual temperature increases or pressure drops—and take corrective action before a system failure occurs.

Challenges in Implementing CPS

While CPS holds great promise, its deployment comes with several challenges:

- **System Complexity**: Designing and maintaining CPS involves coordinating a vast array of sensors, controllers, algorithms, and communication networks. Ensuring these components work harmoniously is a complex task.
- **Security and Privacy**: Given the vast amount of data exchanged in CPS, cybersecurity is a critical concern. Vulnerabilities in communication networks or embedded systems can be exploited by cyber-attacks, potentially disrupting operations and compromising safety.
- **Scalability**: As systems grow in size and complexity, scaling up CPS can be difficult, especially when large networks of sensors or devices are involved.
- **Real-Time Data Processing**: Processing large volumes of sensor data in real-time requires powerful computing resources and advanced algorithms to ensure that the system responds quickly

enough to be effective.

Future Trends in CPS

The future of CPS looks promising with continued advancements in technologies such as:

- **5G Connectivity**: The arrival of 5G technology will enable faster, more reliable communication for CPS, particularly in scenarios requiring low latency, such as real-time control in smart grids.
- **Artificial Intelligence (AI) and Machine Learning (ML)**: AI and ML will enable CPS to become even more autonomous by allowing systems to learn from historical data, detect patterns, and optimize system performance over time.
- **Quantum Computing**: Quantum computing holds the potential to significantly enhance the computational capabilities of CPS, particularly in solving complex optimization problems in real-time.

Cyber-Physical Systems are the backbone of modern intelligent infrastructures, from smart grids and renewable energy systems to predictive maintenance and autonomous decision-making. In electrical engineering, CPS represents a convergence of the physical and digital worlds, allowing systems to continuously adapt, self-optimize, and predict failures before they occur. Despite challenges related to security, complexity, and scalability, CPS will continue to evolve, powered by innovations in AI, edge computing, and 5G technology, making future electrical systems smarter, more resilient, and more efficient.

SIX

ELECTRICAL SYSTEMS AND DIGITAL TWINS

The integration of Digital Twins into electrical systems represents a groundbreaking shift in the way engineers monitor, manage, and optimize power infrastructures. Traditionally, electrical systems have been designed and managed through physical control mechanisms and operational processes, often without the real-time, predictive insights that are now possible with digital technology. However, the advent of Digital Twin technology has radically transformed the landscape of electrical engineering by providing a dynamic, data-driven replica of physical systems in a virtual environment. These virtual models are capable of mirroring the behavior and performance of physical assets—such as transformers, generators, substations, and entire power grids—in real-time.

The Digital Twin concept involves creating an accurate digital replica of a physical object or system, including both its geometry and operational data. For electrical systems, this integration facilitates enhanced monitoring, simulation, and predictive analysis, enabling the digital model to replicate real-world scenarios under various conditions. By merging cyber-physical systems (CPS), IoT sensors, and advanced computational algorithms, Digital Twins bring unparalleled opportunities for performance optimization, fault detection, predictive maintenance, and decision-making in electrical infrastructures. This synergy creates a continuous feedback loop where data from the real world is continuously fed into the digital twin, allowing for real-time insights and more effective management strategies.

Moreover, as electrical systems increasingly incorporate renewable energy sources, distributed generation, and smart grid technologies, the integration of Digital Twins becomes vital for managing the complexity and dynamism of modern power systems. Digital Twins enable engineers to model and simulate energy flow, manage demand-response mechanisms, assess grid resilience, and predict potential issues before they escalate into failures. This proactive approach not only reduces the likelihood of power outages and grid instability but also enhances the efficiency of energy distribution, ensuring a more sustainable and reliable power network.

The integration of Digital Twins into electrical systems is not limited to operational management. The technology plays a pivotal role in optimizing system design, performance validation, and lifecycle management of critical assets. Through real-time data synchronization, performance analytics, and scenario-based simulations, Digital Twins enable the optimization of energy consumption, load balancing, and resource allocation. In addition, predictive maintenance powered by Digital Twins helps identify potential failures or inefficiencies in electrical components before they manifest physically, thereby extending the operational lifespan of equipment and minimizing downtime. The intersection of these two powerful technologies—Digital Twins and electrical systems—ushers in a new era of intelligent infrastructure that is capable of adapting, self-healing, and evolving to meet the demands of a rapidly changing energy landscape.

As we delve deeper into the integration of Digital Twins within electrical systems, this chapter will explore the technological frameworks, key benefits, challenges, and future trends that define this exciting convergence. Through a detailed examination of the architecture, data integration, communication protocols, and real-time control mechanisms, we will uncover how Digital Twin technology is revolutionizing the design, operation, and maintenance of electrical networks. By doing so, we will outline the profound impact this integration is having on improving energy efficiency, reducing operational risks, and paving the way for the development of smart grids, autonomous systems, and sustainable energy solutions in the 21st century.

SMART GRIDS AND POWER SYSTEMS

The modern electricity grid is evolving from a traditional, centralized model into a more sophisticated, intelligent system known as the Smart Grid. This transition is driven by the need for improved efficiency, greater sustainability, better integration of renewable energy sources, and enhanced reliability. The concept of a Smart Grid goes beyond simply automating the power network; it represents a comprehensive system that uses advanced communication, sensor technologies, data analytics, and automated decision-making to optimize the generation, distribution, and consumption of electricity in real-time.

A Smart Grid is not just an advanced version of the electrical grid but a cyber-physical system that integrates digital technologies with physical power infrastructure. It enables two-way communication between utilities and consumers, allowing for real-time monitoring and control of electricity flow, enhanced grid reliability, and more efficient energy use. This interconnectedness between physical devices and digital control systems is what allows the grid to become "smart."

Smart Grids enable more dynamic and flexible management of electrical systems, facilitating the integration of distributed energy resources (DERs), such as solar panels, wind turbines, and battery storage, into the grid. They can respond quickly to fluctuations in demand, reroute electricity, manage outages, and enhance overall system resilience. This transformation is essential as electrical grids become more complex, with an increasing reliance on renewable energy sources, electric vehicles, and decentralized power generation.

Key Features of Smart Grids

Smart Grids are distinguished from traditional grids by several advanced features that enhance their functionality, reliability, and efficiency. These features include:

Two-Way Communication

One of the key features of a Smart Grid is the ability to allow bi-directional communication between utilities and consumers. In traditional grids, communication is one-way, with power flowing from central plants to consumers. However, Smart Grids allow real-time information exchange on both supply and demand sides of the system. For instance, utilities can send commands to appliances (like smart meters) to reduce power consumption during peak hours, while consumers can communicate their energy usage preferences. This communication is enabled through advanced communication protocols, such as fiber optics, wireless technologies, and 5G.

Advanced Metering Infrastructure (AMI)

Advanced Metering Infrastructure refers to the systems that include smart meters and data collection devices that allow for real-time measurement and reporting of electricity usage. Smart meters enable both consumers and utilities to monitor energy consumption on an hourly or minute-by-minute basis. This granular data helps consumers make informed decisions about their energy usage while allowing utilities to better forecast demand, detect faults, and balance the load efficiently. With demand response capabilities, consumers can also reduce their energy costs by shifting usage to off-peak times, contributing to overall grid stability.

Real-Time Monitoring and Control

The use of sensors, IoT devices, and data analytics in Smart Grids enables real-time monitoring of electrical parameters such as voltage, current, power quality, and frequency. With continuous data collection from the grid's physical components (such as transformers, circuit breakers, and lines), utilities can monitor the health of their equipment and detect irregularities or faults almost instantaneously. This enables rapid fault detection, prevention, and restoration of services, minimizing downtime and enhancing grid reliability. Additionally, automated control systems can quickly reroute power in the event of faults, ensuring that services remain uninterrupted.

Distributed Generation and Energy Storage

Smart Grids are designed to support the integration of distributed energy resources (DERs) such as solar panels, wind turbines, and battery storage systems. This enables greater flexibility in energy generation and consumption. Unlike traditional grids that rely heavily on centralized power generation, Smart Grids allow for electricity to be generated at various points across the network. These decentralized sources of energy can be seamlessly integrated and balanced to ensure a steady supply of power to the grid.

Energy storage systems, like lithium-ion batteries and pumped hydro storage, are also a critical component of Smart Grids. These systems store excess energy generated during periods of low demand and release it when demand peaks. This helps to smooth out the intermittent nature of renewable energy sources (such as solar or wind), which are subject to fluctuations.

Self-Healing and Fault Tolerance

A key feature of Smart Grids is their ability to self-heal in the event of faults or failures. By leveraging advanced control systems, sensors, and automated switching mechanisms, Smart Grids can detect faults (such as downed power lines or overloaded transformers) and automatically reroute electricity to unaffected areas. This minimizes disruptions and speeds up restoration times. Predictive analytics and machine learning algorithms can also identify potential system failures before they occur, allowing for preventive maintenance and avoiding costly outages.

Role of Digital Twin in Smart Grid Integration

Digital Twins play an essential role in the development and operation of Smart Grids by providing a virtual representation of the grid's infrastructure and operational dynamics. A Digital Twin in the context of Smart Grids is a detailed digital model that mirrors the physical network's components, performance, and behavior in real-time. It continuously updates as new data is collected from sensors and meters embedded throughout the grid.

a. Real-Time Grid Simulation

Digital Twins enable engineers to simulate different operational conditions and test various scenarios without interrupting the physical grid. For example, engineers can model the effect of introducing a new renewable energy source, or the potential consequences of a fault at a specific location. These simulations help utilities make better-informed decisions and plan for a range of possible outcomes, reducing the risk of system failures.

b. Predictive Maintenance

Using the real-time data fed into the Digital Twin, utilities can perform predictive maintenance by forecasting when grid equipment (transformers, circuit breakers, etc.) is likely to fail or need servicing. This predictive capability reduces the need for reactive maintenance and ensures that the grid operates efficiently. By analyzing historical data trends and equipment performance, the system can suggest optimal maintenance schedules, extending the lifespan of critical infrastructure and reducing downtime.

c. Load Forecasting and Energy Optimization

Digital Twins can enhance load forecasting by simulating energy demand over time, considering various factors such as weather, holidays, economic activity, and consumer behavior. This allows utilities to optimize energy distribution and avoid overloading the grid during peak times. Through this simulation, the system can propose real-time adjustments, such as demand-side management strategies, to balance the supply and demand of electricity.

d. Integration of Renewable Energy

Renewable energy sources like solar and wind have inherent variability in their generation patterns. By integrating Digital Twins, the grid can better forecast renewable energy production and adapt to fluctuating conditions. A Digital Twin model can simulate how the grid will respond to changing renewable inputs, balancing energy production with demand. The model can also assist in optimizing the use of storage systems to ensure that excess renewable energy is captured and used effectively.

3. Benefits of Smart Grids

a. Enhanced Efficiency and Reliability

Smart Grids enhance the efficiency of power generation, transmission, and consumption by using real-time data to manage electricity flow. By dynamically adjusting the power distribution based on current demand, Smart Grids help utilities reduce energy loss and avoid waste. Furthermore, real-time monitoring enables quicker responses to faults, improving grid reliability and preventing long-term outages.

b. Sustainability and Reduced Carbon Footprint

One of the driving forces behind the development of Smart Grids is the integration of renewable energy sources. By enabling the efficient distribution of solar, wind, and hydroelectric power, Smart Grids help reduce the reliance on fossil fuels, contributing to lower greenhouse gas emissions. Moreover, demand-response programs, facilitated by the Smart Grid's real-time data collection, enable consumers to reduce their energy usage during peak periods, further optimizing energy use and promoting sustainability.

c. Economic Benefits

The integration of Smart Grids brings about significant economic benefits for both consumers and utilities. For consumers, Smart Grids provide more accurate billing, better control over energy consumption, and the ability to save money through time-of-use pricing models. For utilities, they enable more efficient resource management, reduce operational costs, and extend the life of grid assets.

d. Consumer Empowerment

Smart Grids give consumers more control over their energy consumption. With real-time data available through smart meters and home energy management systems, consumers can make more informed decisions about when and how to use electricity. For example, households can use smart appliances to optimize energy use during off-peak hours, contributing to overall grid stability and reducing their energy bills.

Challenges and Future of Smart Grids

While Smart Grids offer numerous advantages, their widespread adoption presents several challenges:

a. Cybersecurity

The increased connectivity in Smart Grids opens them up to potential cyber-attacks. Ensuring the security of communication networks, data storage, and control systems is paramount to maintaining the integrity of the grid.

b. Data Privacy

The vast amounts of real-time data collected by Smart Grids raise concerns about data privacy. Ensuring that consumer data is protected from unauthorized access and misuse is a critical issue that must be addressed.

c. Integration Complexity

Integrating renewable energy sources, energy storage, and other distributed resources into existing grid infrastructure is a complex process that requires careful planning, coordination, and investment. The challenge lies in ensuring that these components work seamlessly together to maintain grid stability.

d. Regulatory and Policy Issues

The development and deployment of Smart Grids require clear and consistent regulatory frameworks that address issues such as data governance, energy pricing, and grid modernization. Policymakers must create standards that promote innovation while ensuring system reliability and fairness.

Smart Grids are poised to revolutionize the way electricity is generated, distributed, and consumed. Through the integration of advanced digital technologies, real-time monitoring, and automated control, Smart Grids provide greater efficiency, sustainability, and resilience for modern electrical systems. The integration of Digital Twins further enhances these capabilities by providing a virtual representation of the grid, enabling predictive maintenance, optimized energy use, and improved decision-making. As Smart Grids continue to evolve, they will play a critical role in facilitating the transition to a more sustainable, reliable, and responsive energy infrastructure.

ELECTRIC MACHINES AND DRIVES

Electric machines and drives are the backbone of many modern industrial applications, playing a pivotal role in converting electrical energy into mechanical energy and vice versa. These technologies are essential for a wide range of industries, including power generation, automotive, manufacturing, robotics, and transportation. The integration of electric machines, such as motors, generators, and transformers, with drives (the electronic systems that control their operation) forms the foundation for efficient, precise, and flexible power control in numerous applications.

At the core of electrical engineering and industrial automation, electric machines convert energy from one form to another. Electric motors convert electrical energy into mechanical work, while generators perform the opposite, converting mechanical energy into electrical energy. The performance of these machines is significantly influenced by the type of drives used to control them. Electric drives, consisting of power electronics and control systems, provide the necessary mechanisms to operate electric machines efficiently, with precise speed, torque, and position control.

Types of Electric Machines

Electric machines come in various types, each designed for specific applications. These include DC motors, AC motors, synchronous motors, induction motors, permanent magnet motors, and stepper motors. Each machine has its own advantages, depending on the application requirements such as speed control, efficiency, size, and cost.

a. DC Motors

DC motors are one of the simplest types of electric motors, where the rotation of the motor is generated by the interaction between a magnetic field and the current flowing through the armature. DC motors offer excellent speed control and are commonly used in applications requiring precise speed regulation, such as in electric vehicles (EVs), robotics, and small appliances.

- Applications: EVs, robotics, conveyor belts, and small appliances.
- Advantages: Simple control, high torque at low speeds, precise speed regulation.
- Disadvantages: Maintenance due to brushes and commutators, limited efficiency at higher speeds.

b. AC Motors

AC motors are powered by alternating current, and they are the most commonly used motors in industrial applications due to their robustness, reliability, and simple construction. There are two primary types of AC motors: synchronous and induction motors.

- Synchronous Motors: The rotor in a synchronous motor rotates at the same speed as the rotating magnetic field. These motors are commonly used in applications where a precise speed is required, such as in power plants.

  - Applications: Power plants, synchronous generators.
  - Advantages: Precise speed control, high efficiency.

- Induction Motors: These are the most widely used type of AC motor. In an induction motor, the current in the rotor is induced by the rotating magnetic field of the stator. Induction motors are simple, reliable, and inexpensive, but they lack precise speed control unless driven by a variable frequency drive (VFD).

- ◦ Applications: Pumps, fans, conveyors, HVAC systems, household appliances.
- ◦ Advantages: Simplicity, low cost, high reliability.
- ◦ Disadvantages: Fixed speed (unless VFD is used), lower efficiency under varying load conditions.

c. Permanent Magnet Motors (PMM)

Permanent magnet motors are typically used in applications that require high efficiency and compact design. These motors use magnets to create the magnetic field, which eliminates the need for an external power source for the field. The use of permanent magnets in the rotor reduces energy losses, making these motors more efficient compared to their induction counterparts.

- Applications: Electric vehicles (EVs), robotics, small appliances, and HVAC systems.
- Advantages: Higher efficiency, compact design, reduced energy consumption.
- Disadvantages: High cost of permanent magnets, limited torque at lower speeds.

d. Stepper Motors

Stepper motors are electric motors that move in discrete steps. These motors are primarily used in applications requiring precise control of position, such as in 3D printers, CNC machines, and robotics. The ability to control the motor's rotation in precise increments makes stepper motors ideal for applications where accuracy and repeatability are critical.

- Applications: 3D printers, CNC machines, camera positioning, robotics.
- Advantages: Precise control of position and speed, no feedback system required.
- Disadvantages: Lower efficiency, can generate heat at high speeds.

Electric Drives and Their Control

Electric drives are systems that control the operation of electric machines, providing flexibility in their speed, torque, and position control. The drive system consists of several components, including a controller, a power converter, and sometimes a feedback system. Electric drives are particularly important in industrial automation and are used to optimize the performance of electric machines for energy efficiency, reliability, and precision.

Components of Electric Drives

1. Power Converter: The power converter is responsible for converting electrical power from the supply into a form suitable for the motor. Depending on the type of motor and the application, this could involve DC-AC conversion (in the case of AC motors), or controlling the DC voltage (in the case of DC motors). Power converters include inverters, rectifiers, and choppers.
2. Controller: The controller is responsible for processing inputs (such as speed, torque, or position demands) and sending commands to the power converter to control the electric machine. Advanced controllers use feedback loops from the machine to ensure precise operation.
3. Feedback Systems: Feedback systems, such as encoders or tachometers, are used to monitor the machine's output (speed, torque, position) and provide real-time data to the controller, ensuring the motor operates at the desired parameters.

Types of Drives

1. DC Drives: DC drives control the operation of DC motors, typically used in applications that require fine speed control. DC drives are simple and offer good performance in small, low-power systems, but they require maintenance due to the brushes and commutators.

2. AC Drives: AC drives (also known as variable frequency drives (VFDs)) are used to control the speed of AC motors. By adjusting the frequency of the power supplied to the motor, VFDs allow for precise speed control, energy savings, and protection against motor overloads.

3. Servo Drives: Servo drives are used in servo motors, which are designed for high-precision applications. These drives are often used in robotics, CNC machines, and other applications requiring precise position control. Servo drives typically operate in closed-loop systems, using feedback mechanisms to ensure accurate control.

4. Brushless DC Drives (BLDC): These drives are used for brushless DC motors, which have higher efficiency and require less maintenance than traditional DC motors. BLDC motors are commonly used in applications such as drones, electric vehicles, and medical equipment.

Applications of Electric Machines and Drives

The integration of electric machines and drives spans across a wide array of applications. These systems provide the necessary performance and precision for industries ranging from manufacturing to transportation, agriculture, and beyond.

Industrial Automation and Manufacturing

Electric drives are integral to industrial automation systems, enabling precise control of motors in applications such as conveyor belts, pumps, fans, and assembly lines. Variable frequency drives (VFDs) and servo drives are used to optimize motor performance, energy efficiency, and system flexibility in these applications.

- Applications: Conveyor systems, pumps, fans, lifts, robotics, CNC machines.
- Benefits: Increased productivity, reduced downtime, improved energy efficiency.

Electric Vehicles (EVs)

Electric machines and drives are central to the operation of electric vehicles (EVs). Motors such as permanent magnet synchronous motors (PMSMs) or induction motors are used to drive the wheels, while inverters and DC-DC converters manage the power between the battery and motor. The use of electric drives enables efficient speed control, torque management, and regenerative braking.

- Applications: Electric cars, buses, electric trucks, electric bicycles.
- Benefits: Reduced carbon footprint, lower operating costs, smooth and efficient operation.

Renewable Energy Systems

Electric machines, including generators and wind turbines, play a significant role in renewable energy systems. Wind turbines, for example, use synchronous generators to convert mechanical energy from wind into electrical energy. Solar inverters are used to convert DC power from solar panels into AC power suitable for grid integration.

- Applications: Wind farms, solar power systems, hydropower generation.
- Benefits: Clean energy generation, reduced environmental impact, sustainability.

Robotics and Automation

Electric motors and drives are essential in robotics, where precision and reliability are critical. Motors like stepper motors or servo motors are used to control movement, position, and speed in robotic arms, drones, and automated systems.

- Applications: Industrial robots, drones, medical robots, automated assembly systems.

- Benefits: Precision, reliability, flexibility in manufacturing processes.

Future Trends in Electric Machines and Drives

The future of electric machines and drives is shaped by ongoing advancements in power electronics, control algorithms, and material science. Some key trends include:

a. Integration with Smart Grids

Electric machines and drives are expected to become more integrated with smart grid technologies, where advanced sensor networks and communication protocols enable more dynamic control over energy usage and load balancing. Drives will be able to interact with the grid in real-time, adjusting power consumption based on grid demand.

b. Electrification of Transportation

The growing demand for electric vehicles (EVs), including electric trucks, electric buses, and electric planes, will drive the development of more efficient motors and drives, capable of providing higher performance with smaller and lighter designs.

c. Energy Efficiency Improvements

The focus on improving energy efficiency will continue to push advancements in motor design, drive systems, and power conversion technologies. Efficient electric machines and drives will be crucial in reducing global energy consumption and carbon emissions, especially in sectors like manufacturing and transportation.

Electric machines and drives are integral to the functioning of modern industrial systems and the transition toward more sustainable and energy-efficient technologies. With their ability to convert electrical energy into mechanical work and provide precise control over operations, these systems enable efficient automation, precise positioning, and reliable performance across a wide array of applications. As technology continues to advance, electric machines and drives will evolve to meet the challenges of energy efficiency, system integration, and the demand for smarter, more flexible industrial and consumer systems.

RENEWABLE ENERGY SYSTEMS

Renewable energy systems are technologies designed to harness energy from renewable sources such as the sun, wind, water, geothermal heat, and biomass. These systems have become central to global efforts to reduce greenhouse gas emissions, combat climate change, and create a sustainable energy future. As the world transitions from fossil fuels to cleaner, more sustainable alternatives, renewable energy systems are becoming increasingly integral in power generation, transportation, and industrial applications.

Types of Renewable Energy Systems

Renewable energy systems can be categorized based on the type of energy they harvest. The four most prominent sources are solar, wind, hydropower, and biomass, each of which has its own set of technologies and advantages

Solar Energy Systems

Solar energy systems capture energy from sunlight and convert it into electricity or heat. These systems are among the fastest-growing sources of renewable energy due to their scalability, cost-effectiveness, and the abundance of sunlight in many regions.

1. Photovoltaic (PV) Solar Systems: These systems use solar panels made up of semiconductor materials (usually silicon) to convert sunlight directly into electricity. PV solar systems are widely used in residential, commercial, and utility-scale applications.

   - Applications: Residential solar panels, large-scale solar farms, solar-powered buildings.
   - Benefits: Clean, abundant, scalable, minimal maintenance, and low operating costs.
   - Challenges: Intermittency due to weather and time of day, need for energy storage to provide continuous power.

2. Solar Thermal Systems: These systems use mirrors or lenses to concentrate sunlight onto a receiver, which then heats up a fluid to produce steam. The steam drives a turbine connected to a generator, converting heat into electricity.

   - Applications: Concentrated solar power (CSP) plants, industrial heat applications.
   - Benefits: High efficiency in sunny regions, can store heat for later use.
   - Challenges: High capital cost, location-specific (best in regions with consistent sunlight).

Wind Energy Systems

Wind energy systems convert the kinetic energy of wind into electrical energy using wind turbines. Wind power is one of the most mature and rapidly expanding sources of renewable energy globally, particularly in areas with consistent and strong wind patterns.

1. Onshore Wind Turbines: These are installed on land and are the most common type of wind energy system. They range in size from small, residential-scale turbines to large, utility-scale systems that can power thousands of homes.

   - Applications: Wind farms on land, residential wind turbines.
   - Benefits: Clean energy source, low operating costs once installed.
   - Challenges: Noise, visual impact, land usage, and intermittency (wind not always available).

2. Offshore Wind Turbines: Installed in bodies of water, typically on the continental shelf, offshore turbines take advantage of stronger, more consistent winds. These systems can be more expensive to install due to the complexity of offshore construction but can produce much more power.

- ○ Applications: Offshore wind farms.
- ○ Benefits: Stronger and more consistent wind, higher energy yield.
- ○ Challenges: High installation costs, potential environmental impact on marine ecosystems.

Hydropower Systems

Hydropower, or hydroelectric power, generates electricity by converting the energy of flowing water into mechanical energy through turbines. It is one of the oldest and most reliable forms of renewable energy, with large-scale hydropower providing a significant portion of the world's renewable electricity.

1. Run-of-River Hydropower: This type of hydropower system harnesses the natural flow of rivers without requiring large dams. It is a more environmentally friendly option compared to traditional hydropower, which can disrupt local ecosystems.

   - ○ Applications: Small to medium-sized river-based power plants.
   - ○ Benefits: Less environmental impact, relatively low cost.
   - ○ Challenges: Limited to regions with adequate river flow, seasonal variability.

2. Pumped Storage Hydropower: This system involves storing energy by pumping water from a lower reservoir to an upper one when there is excess electricity available. When demand is high, the water is released to generate electricity. This system acts as a form of energy storage and helps balance supply and demand.

   - ○ Applications: Large-scale energy storage, grid balancing.
   - ○ Benefits: Provides grid stability, energy storage capacity.
   - ○ Challenges: Requires significant infrastructure, potential environmental impact.

3. Tidal and Wave Energy: These forms of hydropower use the energy from tidal movements and ocean waves to generate electricity. Tidal energy systems typically use underwater turbines, while wave energy systems capture the motion of waves to drive generators.

   - Applications: Coastal areas with high tidal and wave activity.
   - Benefits: Predictable and reliable energy source.
   - Challenges: High cost, environmental and technological challenges, limited geographic suitability.

Biomass Energy Systems

Biomass energy involves converting organic materials—such as wood, agricultural waste, or dedicated energy crops—into electricity, heat, or biofuels. Biomass can be burned directly to produce heat or converted into biogas or biofuels through chemical processes.

1. Biomass Power Plants: These plants burn organic materials to generate heat, which is then used to produce steam that drives a turbine connected to a generator. Biomass power plants are often co-located with industries that produce waste materials like wood products or agriculture.

   - Applications: Waste-to-energy plants, combined heat and power (CHP) systems.
   - Benefits: Utilizes waste materials, reduces landfill use, renewable fuel source.
   - Challenges: Emissions from burning, land-use competition, supply chain logistics.

2. Biogas Production: Biogas is produced through the anaerobic digestion of organic waste, such as manure, food waste, and sewage. The resulting methane gas can be used to generate electricity or as a vehicle fuel.

- Applications: Biogas plants, agricultural waste management, energy production.
- Benefits: Reduces methane emissions from waste, produces renewable energy, low-cost fuel.
- Challenges: Needs specialized infrastructure, emissions from process if not managed.

Integration of Renewable Energy with Power Systems

The integration of renewable energy systems with existing power grids poses unique challenges and opportunities. Since renewable energy sources like solar and wind are intermittent, grid operators must balance supply and demand while ensuring the stability of the grid. The challenge is to ensure that the variability of renewable energy does not compromise the reliability of the electrical system.

Smart Grids and Energy Storage

Smart grids are modernized electrical grids that use digital communication technology to monitor and manage the distribution of electricity from various sources, including renewables. Smart grids help to integrate renewable energy by enabling real-time management of energy generation and consumption. Additionally, energy storage technologies such as batteries, pumped hydro storage, and thermal storage are critical to storing excess energy generated during periods of high renewable output and dispatching it when demand is high or renewable generation is low.

- Applications: Grid balancing, energy storage systems, real-time energy management.
- Benefits: Increased reliability, better integration of renewables, real-time response to grid needs.

Distributed Energy Resources (DERs)

Renewable energy systems can also be integrated as distributed energy resources (DERs), where power generation occurs closer to the point of use rather than at centralized plants. This includes rooftop solar panels, small-scale wind turbines, and biomass digesters. DERs provide the potential for decentralized power generation and greater resilience against grid outages.

- Applications: Residential solar, community-based wind farms, local biomass plants.
- Benefits: Increased energy resilience, reduced transmission losses, empowerment of local communities.

Microgrids

A microgrid is a small-scale energy system that can operate independently from the main grid. Microgrids integrate various renewable energy sources with storage systems and can provide energy security for critical infrastructure, such as hospitals, military bases, and remote communities.

- Applications: Remote communities, emergency backup systems, university campuses.
- Benefits: Energy independence, increased resilience, integration of renewable energy in off-grid areas.

Challenges and Opportunities

While renewable energy systems offer significant environmental and economic benefits, there are still challenges associated with their widespread adoption.

a. Intermittency and Reliability

Since many renewable energy sources (such as solar and wind) are intermittent, there is variability in the energy they produce. This creates challenges in ensuring a stable and reliable supply of electricity. Advanced forecasting, energy storage, and demand-response technologies are crucial to addressing these challenges.

b. Infrastructure and Cost

The infrastructure required to integrate renewable energy systems into the grid can be expensive, especially in regions that lack the necessary transmission networks or energy storage capabilities. Additionally, the initial cost of installing renewable energy systems (such as wind turbines or solar panels) can be high, though prices have been decreasing over time.

c. Environmental and Social Impact

While renewable energy systems have a much lower environmental impact compared to fossil fuels, they can still have localized impacts. For example, large hydropower projects can disrupt local ecosystems and communities, while wind turbines can affect bird populations. Careful planning and environmental assessments are needed to minimize these impacts.

Renewable energy systems are fundamental to the transition to a more sustainable and resilient global energy system. By harnessing the power of natural resources like the sun, wind, water, and biomass, these systems offer a clean, reliable, and increasingly cost-effective way to generate electricity and heat. However, challenges related to intermittency, infrastructure, and environmental impacts must be addressed to fully realize the potential of renewable energy. As technology continues to improve and costs continue to fall, renewable energy will play an increasingly central role in global energy production, helping to mitigate climate change and ensure a sustainable energy future.

BUILDING AUTOMATION AND ENERGY MANAGEMENT

Building Automation and Energy Management systems are integral in optimizing energy consumption, improving efficiency, and reducing environmental impact in both residential and commercial settings. These systems use advanced technologies, such as sensors, controls, and data analytics, to manage building operations, including heating, ventilation, air conditioning (HVAC), lighting, security, and energy usage. The goal is to create a comfortable, safe, and energy-efficient environment for occupants while minimizing operational costs and maximizing resource efficiency.

Building Automation Systems (BAS)

A Building Automation System (BAS) is a network of hardware and software designed to control and monitor the building's critical systems automatically. BAS integrates various building functions, including heating, cooling, lighting, and security, into a unified system. These systems not only ensure optimal comfort and safety for building occupants but also help maintain energy efficiency and improve overall operational effectiveness.

a. Components of Building Automation Systems

1. **Sensors**: Sensors measure various parameters such as temperature, humidity, light levels, occupancy, air quality, and motion. These data points are crucial in regulating systems like HVAC and lighting to maintain comfort while optimizing energy usage.

   - Examples: Temperature sensors for HVAC control, light sensors for automatic dimming, occupancy sensors for lighting control.
   - Benefits: Real-time data collection for adaptive system responses, improved energy efficiency.

2. **Controllers**: Controllers receive input from sensors and manage the operation of systems such as HVAC, lighting, and alarms. These devices process information from sensors and make decisions to adjust settings based on pre-programmed or real-time data.

   - Examples: Programmable controllers for HVAC temperature regulation, lighting control modules.
   - Benefits: Automated decision-making reduces manual intervention, streamlines operations.

3. **Actuators**: Actuators are devices that respond to controller signals to physically adjust systems, such as adjusting the flow of air in HVAC systems or opening and closing windows for

ventilation.

- ○ Examples: Dampers in HVAC systems, electric valves in water-based systems.
- ○ Benefits: Enables precise adjustments in building systems to maintain optimal conditions.

4. **User Interface**: The user interface allows building managers or facility operators to interact with the automation system. It may include a graphical interface for monitoring performance, adjusting system parameters, and reviewing historical data.

- ○ Examples: Building management software, mobile apps for remote control.
- ○ Benefits: Provides users with easy access to control settings, data visualizations, and system status reports.

Energy Management Systems (EMS)

Energy Management Systems (EMS) are designed to optimize energy consumption within a building by monitoring energy use, identifying inefficiencies, and implementing strategies to reduce energy costs. An EMS works in conjunction with BAS by leveraging data from sensors and controllers to manage energy resources more effectively. The goal is to balance energy use with comfort needs while minimizing waste.

Key Functions of Energy Management Systems

Energy Monitoring and Analytics: EMS continuously collects and analyzes data on energy consumption from various building systems (HVAC, lighting, appliances). This allows building operators to detect inefficiencies and high-energy usage patterns, enabling informed decision-making.

- ○ Applications: Real-time energy tracking, peak load identification, consumption forecasting.

- Benefits: Improved visibility into energy usage, data-driven insights for decision-making.

Load Management: EMS helps optimize the load on electrical systems by reducing demand during peak times or managing the usage of heavy equipment in a way that prevents overloading the grid or causing spikes in energy costs. This can include turning off or reducing power to non-essential systems during peak hours.

- Applications: Peak shaving, demand response programs, automated load shifting.
- Benefits: Lower energy costs, improved grid stability, and efficient load distribution.

Energy Consumption Forecasting: Using historical data and predictive analytics, EMS can forecast future energy consumption patterns. This can help building operators plan energy usage more effectively, reduce unnecessary consumption, and prevent energy waste.

- Applications: Predictive analytics, demand forecasting.
- Benefits: Better resource planning, proactive energy usage management.

Energy Efficiency Optimization: By integrating advanced algorithms, EMS can recommend and implement measures to improve building energy efficiency. This can include optimizing HVAC settings, using energy-efficient lighting, and upgrading insulation or windows.

- Applications: Optimization of building energy systems, energy-efficient lighting and HVAC controls.
- Benefits: Reduced operational costs, lower energy bills, and enhanced sustainability.

Integration with Renewable Energy: EMS can help integrate renewable energy sources such as solar panels or wind turbines into the building's energy system. This allows buildings to become partially or fully self-sufficient in terms of energy supply, reducing reliance on external grids.

- Applications: Solar power integration, wind turbine integration, energy storage systems.
- Benefits: Reduced carbon footprint, lower dependence on fossil fuels, increased energy security.

Advanced Technologies in Building Automation and Energy Management

To enhance the functionality of BAS and EMS, several advanced technologies are being integrated into building automation systems. These technologies allow for greater energy efficiency, automation, and predictive capabilities, helping buildings achieve higher levels of sustainability and reduced operational costs.

a. Artificial Intelligence (AI) and Machine Learning (ML)

AI and machine learning can analyze vast amounts of data generated by building sensors to detect patterns, predict energy consumption, and optimize system performance. AI algorithms can automatically adjust heating, cooling, and lighting systems based on real-time occupancy data and environmental conditions, making buildings smarter and more energy-efficient.

- Applications: Predictive maintenance, demand response, energy optimization.
- Benefits: Proactive system adjustments, enhanced building intelligence, cost savings through automation.

b. Internet of Things (IoT)

IoT devices connect various building systems and allow them to communicate with each other, sharing real-time data to optimize performance. IoT-enabled smart meters, sensors, and devices give building managers continuous visibility into energy consumption and system performance.

- Applications: Smart thermostats, intelligent lighting systems, connected HVAC devices.
- Benefits: Real-time monitoring, remote control, better energy insights.

c. Cloud Computing

Cloud computing platforms enable the storage, analysis, and sharing of large volumes of building data. Cloud-based energy management platforms offer centralized control and monitoring of multiple buildings, allowing operators to manage energy consumption across entire portfolios in real-time.

- Applications: Remote energy management, cloud-based analytics, centralized control.
- Benefits: Scalability, remote monitoring, improved collaboration.

d. Advanced Energy Storage Systems

Energy storage technologies, such as batteries and thermal storage, play a crucial role in balancing energy supply and demand. These systems store excess energy during periods of low demand (e.g., at night or during sunny weather) and discharge it during peak periods or when renewable energy sources are unavailable.

- Applications: Solar energy storage, demand response, grid balancing.
- Benefits: Increased energy reliability, reduced costs, improved integration with renewable energy.

4. Benefits of Building Automation and Energy Management

The integration of building automation and energy management systems offers a wide array of benefits for building owners, operators, and occupants, contributing to energy efficiency, cost savings, and sustainability goals.

Energy Efficiency and Cost Savings

By automating building systems and continuously optimizing energy consumption, BAS and EMS significantly reduce energy waste and lower operational costs. The real-time adjustments made by these systems help ensure that energy is used only when needed, resulting in lower energy bills.

Improved Environmental Sustainability

Building automation systems contribute to sustainability by reducing energy consumption and lowering greenhouse gas emissions. By incorporating renewable energy sources and enhancing energy efficiency, buildings can significantly reduce their carbon footprint.

Enhanced Comfort and Safety

Automated systems ensure that building environments remain comfortable for occupants at all times. Heating, cooling, and lighting adjustments are made based on occupancy and environmental conditions, improving the overall comfort level. Additionally, security systems integrated into BAS can enhance occupant safety through automated monitoring and alarm systems.

Regulatory Compliance and Incentives

Many regions have regulations aimed at reducing energy consumption and improving building performance. BAS and EMS help buildings comply with these regulations by monitoring energy usage, ensuring energy-efficient operations, and reporting data in a standardized format. In addition, many governments offer financial incentives and rebates for buildings that adopt energy-efficient technologies, further reducing costs.

Challenges and Future Prospects

While building automation and energy management systems offer significant benefits, there are also challenges to their implementation and widespread adoption.

a. High Initial Costs

The upfront costs of installing advanced BAS and EMS can be substantial, particularly for retrofitting existing buildings. These costs can be a barrier for small and medium-sized businesses and residential properties.

b. Complexity and Integration

Integrating various technologies and systems within a building, particularly when dealing with legacy systems, can be complex. Ensuring seamless integration between different equipment and systems is crucial to maximizing the benefits of BAS and EMS.

c. Data Security and Privacy Concerns

As building systems become increasingly connected, data security and privacy concerns grow. Protecting sensitive data related to energy usage, occupancy patterns, and personal preferences is essential to ensure the system's integrity.

Building Automation and Energy Management systems are critical tools for reducing energy consumption, improving operational efficiency, and enhancing sustainability in modern buildings. By utilizing advanced technologies like AI, IoT, and cloud computing, these systems offer intelligent, real-time solutions that help buildings achieve energy efficiency goals and reduce their environmental impact. However, challenges related to costs, integration, and security need to be addressed to unlock their full potential. As technologies evolve and become more accessible, building automation and energy management will continue to play an essential role in creating smarter, more energy-efficient buildings for the future.

POWER ELECTRONICS AND CONTROL SYSTEMS

Power electronics and control systems play a pivotal role in modern electrical engineering, enabling efficient and reliable operation of electrical systems and devices. They are essential in converting, controlling, and conditioning electrical power to meet the specific requirements of various applications. Power electronics involve the conversion of electrical power from one form to another, while control systems manage and optimize the operation of electrical devices and systems to achieve desired performance outcomes. Together, they contribute significantly to the advancement of technologies in renewable energy systems, electric vehicles, industrial automation, and other critical applications

Power Electronics Overview

Power electronics refers to the application of solid-state electronics to control and convert electrical power efficiently. The field includes the study of devices, circuits, and systems used to convert, control, and condition electrical energy. Power electronics focuses on systems that manage high-power electrical signals, with the primary goal of improving efficiency, performance, and reliability.

a. Types of Power Conversion

The core function of power electronics is the conversion of electrical power from one form to another. This can involve converting AC to DC (rectification), DC to AC (inversion), or adjusting voltage levels (step-up or step-down conversion). The following are the main types of power conversion in power electronics:

1. AC to DC Conversion (Rectification): This process involves converting alternating current (AC) to direct current (DC), a common operation for applications like battery charging, power supplies for electronic devices, and electric vehicle (EV) charging.

   - Devices Used: Diodes, thyristors, and transistors.
   - Applications: Power supplies, battery chargers, DC motors.

2. DC to AC Conversion (Inversion): Inverters are used to convert DC into AC. This is commonly used in renewable energy systems, such as solar power systems, where the power generated by solar panels is DC but must be converted to AC to be used in most homes and businesses.

   - Devices Used: IGBTs (Insulated Gate Bipolar Transistors), MOSFETs (Metal-Oxide-Semiconductor Field-Effect Transistors).

- Applications: Solar inverters, wind turbines, grid-connected power systems.

3. **DC to DC Conversion (Buck and Boost Conversion):** This type of power conversion adjusts the voltage levels of a DC signal. Buck converters reduce the voltage, while boost converters increase it. These systems are vital for efficient energy use and power distribution.

   - Devices Used: Transistors, inductors, capacitors.
   - Applications: Power supplies, DC motor drives, battery-operated devices.

4. **AC to AC Conversion (Cycloconversion):** This involves the conversion of one AC signal to another with different frequency or amplitude. Cycloconverters are typically used in applications requiring frequency control.

   - Devices Used: Thyristors, diodes.
   - Applications: Industrial motor drives, power generation systems.

Power Semiconductor Devices

At the heart of power electronics are power semiconductor devices, which are responsible for switching and controlling electrical energy. These devices allow for the efficient conversion of power and have dramatically improved in performance over the years.

1. **Diodes:** Diodes allow current to flow in one direction only, making them essential for rectification.
2. **Thyristors:** Thyristors are used for high-power switching applications. They can handle high voltage and current levels and are commonly used in rectifiers and AC controllers.

3. IGBTs (Insulated Gate Bipolar Transistors): IGBTs combine the benefits of MOSFETs and BJTs (Bipolar Junction Transistors), providing efficient switching with high-voltage capability, making them suitable for medium to high-power applications.

4. MOSFETs (Metal-Oxide-Semiconductor Field-Effect Transistors): MOSFETs are used for fast switching in low- and medium-power applications, such as DC-DC converters and motor control systems.

Control Systems Overview

Control systems are used to manage, command, and regulate the operation of electrical systems and devices. The goal of a control system is to ensure that the system behaves in a predictable and desired manner, following predefined specifications and handling disturbances effectively.

a. Types of Control Systems

1. Open-Loop Control: In an open-loop control system, the output is not fed back into the input for correction. The system operates based on a set input, but there is no feedback mechanism to correct errors in the system's performance.

    ◦ Example: A fan operating at a constant speed without adjustment based on environmental conditions.
    ◦ Applications: Basic electrical heating, non-critical systems where precision is not essential.

2. Closed-Loop Control (Feedback Control): A closed-loop control system adjusts its operation based on feedback from the output. This allows the system to correct deviations from the desired performance and achieve more precise control.

    ◦ Example: A thermostat that adjusts the heating or cooling in a room based on the temperature feedback.

- Applications: Motor speed control, voltage regulation, automated industrial processes.

3. PID Control: The Proportional-Integral-Derivative (PID) controller is a widely used control strategy in which the output is adjusted based on three factors:

   - Proportional: The correction based on the current error.
   - Integral: The correction based on the accumulated past errors.
   - Derivative: The correction based on the rate of change of the error.
   - Applications: Speed control of motors, temperature regulation in HVAC systems, power electronics.

Key Components of Control Systems

1. Sensors: Sensors detect system parameters such as temperature, speed, voltage, and current, providing the necessary feedback for closed-loop control systems.
2. Controllers: Controllers process the information from sensors and compute the necessary correction or adjustment to the system. They may be microcontrollers, programmable logic controllers (PLCs), or digital signal processors (DSPs).
3. Actuators: Actuators are devices that implement the corrective actions suggested by the controller, such as adjusting a valve, changing the speed of a motor, or controlling a power converter.

Power Electronics in Electrical Systems

The application of power electronics in electrical systems is wide-ranging and includes several critical domains, such as industrial automation, power generation, renewable energy, and transportation.

Renewable Energy Systems

Power electronics play an essential role in integrating renewable energy sources into the electrical grid. Solar inverters, wind turbine converters, and grid stabilization systems rely heavily on power electronics to convert and condition the energy produced by renewable sources. Inverters are used to convert DC power from solar panels or wind turbines into AC power suitable for the grid, and power controllers manage the interaction with the grid, ensuring stable and reliable operation.

- Applications: Solar power conversion, wind energy conversion, grid synchronization.

Electric Vehicles (EVs)

Power electronics are crucial in electric vehicle (EV) technology, particularly in the power conversion and control systems for motors and batteries. The energy from the battery is typically in DC form, which must be converted to AC for the induction motors commonly used in EVs. Additionally, power electronics are responsible for controlling the charging process, ensuring safe and efficient battery management.

- Applications: DC-AC inverters, motor controllers, battery chargers.

Industrial Motor Drives

Power electronics enable precise control of industrial motors, allowing for adjustments in speed, torque, and direction. Variable frequency drives (VFDs) are used to control the speed of AC motors by adjusting the frequency of the input voltage. These drives enhance efficiency by ensuring that motors only consume the energy they need.

- Applications: Pump control, conveyor systems, HVAC motor drives.

Advanced Control Strategies in Power Electronics

With the increasing complexity and demands of modern electrical systems, advanced control strategies have been developed to improve the performance and efficiency of power electronics. These strategies include:

a. Adaptive Control: Adaptive control systems dynamically adjust the control parameters to account for changing system dynamics. This is particularly useful in systems where the load or operating conditions fluctuate, such as electric motor drives and renewable energy systems.

b. Fuzzy Logic Control: Fuzzy logic control uses human-like reasoning to make decisions, particularly in systems with uncertainties or non-linear characteristics. It is often used in systems where conventional control methods (such as PID) may struggle to provide accurate performance.

c. Predictive Control: Predictive control uses models of the system to predict future behavior and adjust control actions accordingly. This method is gaining traction in applications where performance optimization over time is critical, such as battery management in electric vehicles or energy storage systems.

Challenges and Future Trends

While power electronics and control systems offer numerous benefits, they also present certain challenges:

a. Efficiency and Thermal Management: As power converters become more efficient, the need for better thermal management increases. High-power systems generate significant heat, which can limit performance and longevity.

b. Reliability and Durability: Power electronics devices, especially semiconductors, are subject to stress from high current and voltage levels. Ensuring their reliability and longevity is crucial for minimizing downtime and repair costs.

c. Integration and Miniaturization: With the growing demand for compact and integrated systems, there is an ongoing effort to reduce the size of power electronic devices and integrate them with other systems, such as motors and controllers, to improve system performance.

Power electronics and control systems are foundational to modern electrical engineering applications, enabling efficient energy conversion, regulation, and optimization. From renewable energy systems to electric vehicles and industrial automation, the role of power electronics and control systems continues to grow, driven by advancements in semiconductor technology, control algorithms, and integration techniques. As the demand for energy efficiency and reliability increases, these systems will play an even more critical role in shaping the future of electrical systems across a wide range of industries.

SEVEN

DEVELOPMENT TOOLS

The successful development, deployment, and operation of Digital Twins (DT) in various industries, including electrical engineering, require the use of sophisticated development tools and platforms. These tools and platforms provide the necessary environments and frameworks for the creation, simulation, integration, and maintenance of Digital Twin models. Digital Twins serve as virtual replicas of physical systems, enabling real-time monitoring, analysis, and optimization, making the choice of appropriate development tools essential for achieving accurate, scalable, and efficient digital representations. Over the years, a wide variety of tools and platforms have emerged, each designed to address specific aspects of Digital Twin development, from 3D modeling and data acquisition to cloud integration and machine learning implementation.

Development tools for Digital Twins are crucial for various phases of the Digital Twin lifecycle, including data acquisition, model creation, system simulation, and decision-making. They support a range of functionalities, such as real-time data synchronization, predictive modeling, optimization, and control of the physical system based on digital insights. Additionally, many platforms provide integrated environments that allow collaboration across various stakeholders—engineers, data scientists, and business decision-makers—facilitating a seamless flow of information and reducing time-to-market for Digital Twin implementations.

With the increasing adoption of the Internet of Things (IoT), Artificial Intelligence (AI), and Machine Learning (ML), the demand for tools that can handle vast amounts of real-time data and complex simulations has risen significantly. Modern development tools enable the creation of intelligent, autonomous Digital Twins that can simulate system behavior, detect anomalies, and predict future performance, contributing to more informed decision-making and the optimization of operations in various industries. These tools also empower the integration of renewable energy systems, smart grids, and other advanced electrical engineering technologies by providing robust simulation environments to validate system behavior before implementation.

As the Digital Twin concept continues to evolve, the range of available development tools and platforms is expanding, offering new capabilities in modeling, visualization, analysis, and decision support. This chapter explores the key development tools and platforms that are driving the Digital Twin revolution, discussing their features, applications, and the role they play in enabling organizations to create efficient, scalable, and reliable Digital Twin models. Through the exploration of these tools, we gain insights into how Digital Twin technology is being integrated into various sectors, including electrical engineering, manufacturing, smart cities, and beyond. Ultimately, these tools and platforms are reshaping how industries approach design, operation, and maintenance, providing a comprehensive and dynamic environment for managing the digital and physical worlds simultaneously.

SOFTWARE AND SIMULATION TOOLS

The development and deployment of Digital Twins (DT) in various industries rely heavily on software and simulation tools. These tools enable engineers, designers, and researchers to create, test, and validate virtual models of physical systems before real-world implementation. In the context of electrical engineering, software and simulation tools play a crucial role in replicating the behavior of electrical systems, components, and processes in a virtual environment. These tools facilitate detailed analysis, optimization, and decision-making, leading to improved system performance, reduced costs, and enhanced operational efficiency.

The role of software and simulation tools in the Digital Twin lifecycle can be broken down into several key areas, including modeling, simulation, real-time data integration, and performance optimization. By combining different tools for each phase, from system design to post-deployment monitoring, Digital Twins can evolve into sophisticated, dynamic models that mimic the real-world system's behavior accurately. Below, we explore some of the key aspects and categories of software and simulation tools used in Digital Twin development.

Modeling Tools for Digital Twins

The first step in creating a Digital Twin is to develop an accurate and detailed model that represents the physical system. Modeling tools are designed to facilitate this process by providing graphical and mathematical environments in which users can define system parameters, components, and relationships. These tools support the creation of both 2D and 3D models, enabling a comprehensive representation of the system's physical structure and operational attributes.

Types of Modeling Tools:

- CAD (Computer-Aided Design) Software: Tools like AutoCAD, SolidWorks, and CATIA are widely used for creating precise 3D models of physical systems, from electrical grids to mechanical components. These tools enable engineers to visualize complex systems and their interactions before constructing them physically. In the case of Digital Twins, CAD software often serves as the foundation for building detailed virtual representations.

- Mathematical and System Modeling Software: Tools such as MATLAB/Simulink, Mathematica, and Maple are commonly used to model the behavior of systems based on mathematical equations. These tools help in simulating the system's dynamics, control strategies, and performance under various conditions. They provide an ideal environment for engineers to design and test algorithms before implementing them on the actual hardware.

Simulation Tools for Virtual Testing

Once the model is created, simulation tools come into play. These tools enable the virtual testing of the system to evaluate its performance, detect faults, and optimize design parameters without the need for physical prototypes. Simulation tools are essential for testing the behavior of Digital Twins under different operational scenarios and predicting system responses to changes in external factors like load fluctuations, temperature variations, and system faults.

Key Simulation Tools:

ANSYS and COMSOL Multiphysics: These software packages are used for simulating the physical phenomena associated with electrical systems, including electromagnetics, thermal effects, fluid dynamics, and structural mechanics. ANSYS is particularly valuable in simulating the electrical and mechanical interactions of power systems, while COMSOL is widely used in multidisciplinary simulations.

PSS®E (Power System Simulator for Engineering): A specialized tool for power systems analysis and simulation, PSS®E is widely used in electrical engineering to model power grids, analyze load flows, and simulate fault conditions. It is an essential tool for creating and testing Digital Twins of electrical grids and ensuring their stability and efficiency under varying conditions.

Opal-RT Technologies: This platform specializes in real-time simulation and hardware-in-the-loop (HIL) testing. It is commonly used in the testing and validation of power electronics, grid integration, and renewable energy systems. By enabling real-time simulations, it ensures that Digital Twins can be synchronized with actual system performance data.

Real-Time Data Integration and Monitoring Tools

A core feature of Digital Twins is their ability to integrate real-time data from physical systems to continuously update the virtual model and reflect the current state of the system. This integration requires robust software platforms that can handle vast amounts of data from IoT sensors, SCADA (Supervisory Control and Data Acquisition) systems, and other data sources in real-time.

Key Data Integration and Monitoring Platforms:

IoT Platforms: Platforms such as ThingWorx, Microsoft Azure IoT, and AWS IoT are essential for integrating real-time data from various sensors and devices within the physical system. These platforms enable seamless communication between the physical system and the Digital Twin, allowing the virtual model to be continuously updated with live data.

SCADA Systems: SCADA software is commonly used in power generation and distribution systems to monitor and control industrial processes. When integrated with Digital Twins, SCADA systems allow for real-time monitoring and control of electrical grids, power plants, and renewable energy systems, ensuring operational efficiency and safety.

Middleware Solutions: Middleware software acts as a bridge between the data sources and the simulation platform, ensuring smooth data flow and synchronization. Examples include RabbitMQ, MQTT, and OPC UA (Unified Architecture), which facilitate secure and reliable data exchange between sensors, models, and analysis platforms.

Optimization and Control Tools

Optimization tools are designed to refine system performance by adjusting parameters to achieve the best possible outcomes. In the context of Digital Twins, optimization is essential for improving energy efficiency, reducing operational costs, and enhancing system reliability. These tools use advanced algorithms to analyze large sets of data and identify the most optimal strategies for system operation.

Optimization Tools:

- Optimization Software: Tools like GAMS (General Algebraic Modeling System) and IBM CPLEX Optimization Studio provide advanced optimization algorithms for solving complex mathematical problems, such as minimizing energy consumption or optimizing load distribution in power systems. These tools can be integrated with Digital Twin models to refine the operation of electrical systems based on real-time data.
- Control System Design Tools: Control systems are essential for maintaining the stability of electrical systems, particularly in power grids and renewable energy integration. Tools such as MATLAB/Simulink, LabVIEW, and Dymola provide environments for designing and testing control strategies for Digital Twins, enabling autonomous decision-making and system optimization.

Cloud-Based Platforms for Scalability and Collaboration

As Digital Twins become more complex and integrated into larger systems, cloud-based platforms play an increasingly important role in managing large datasets, enhancing computational capabilities, and enabling collaboration across global teams. Cloud platforms provide the necessary infrastructure for storing vast amounts of data generated by Digital Twins and facilitate easy access for stakeholders involved in the system's design, operation, and maintenance.

Popular Cloud Platforms:

- Amazon Web Services (AWS): AWS provides a suite of cloud-based tools for creating and managing Digital Twins, including storage solutions, computing power, and machine learning capabilities. AWS IoT Core, for example, helps connect IoT devices with Digital Twin models, enabling real-time monitoring and analysis.

- Microsoft Azure: Azure offers cloud services for building and deploying Digital Twins, including Azure Digital Twins, which is a comprehensive platform for modeling and simulating the behavior of physical assets and systems. It enables users to create complex models of buildings, grids, and industrial systems, with integration capabilities for IoT and AI.

Collaborative Development Tools

In the development of Digital Twins, collaboration among various stakeholders, such as engineers, data scientists, and business analysts, is crucial for ensuring the successful design and implementation of the system. Collaborative tools facilitate communication, version control, and project management, streamlining workflows and ensuring that all team members are on the same page.

Collaboration Tools:

- GitHub and GitLab: These platforms provide version control and collaboration features for managing the development of software and models. They allow teams to work on code and models simultaneously, track changes, and ensure consistency across multiple versions.
- Jira and Confluence: These project management tools enable teams to manage tasks, track progress, and document development processes. They are essential for coordinating large-scale Digital Twin projects and ensuring that all milestones are met.

The role of software and simulation tools in the development of Digital Twins is indispensable. They provide the foundation for modeling, testing, optimizing, and controlling systems that replicate real-world behavior, enabling engineers to make more informed decisions, improve system performance, and reduce risks. With the integration of advanced tools for real-time data processing, cloud computing, and collaborative development, Digital Twins are becoming increasingly capable of managing complex systems and ensuring the efficient operation of industries such as electrical engineering, manufacturing, and energy management. As technology continues to advance, these tools will play an even more critical role in the evolution of Digital Twin systems, supporting the transition to smarter, more sustainable infrastructure worldwide.

HARDWARE PLATFORMS

The success of Digital Twin (DT) technology depends not only on sophisticated software and simulation tools but also on robust hardware platforms that can effectively collect, process, and exchange data in real-time. In the context of electrical engineering and other industries, hardware platforms such as Programmable Logic Controllers (PLCs), Supervisory Control and Data Acquisition (SCADA) systems, and embedded systems play a crucial role in the implementation and operation of Digital Twins. These hardware systems are responsible for interfacing with physical assets, controlling operations, gathering sensor data, and ensuring seamless communication between the physical and digital worlds. Below, we expand on the role and functionalities of these hardware platforms.

Programmable Logic Controllers (PLCs)

Programmable Logic Controllers (PLCs) are industrial digital computers used for automating and controlling electromechanical processes, such as those in manufacturing, power generation, and distribution systems. PLCs are often the heart of industrial control systems (ICS) and are essential for the real-time operation of machinery and processes. In the context of Digital Twins, PLCs are responsible for collecting data from physical assets, executing control commands, and providing real-time feedback to digital models.

Key Features and Functions:

- Data Acquisition: PLCs connect to various sensors and input devices in the physical system (e.g., temperature, pressure, voltage sensors) to collect real-time data. This data is transmitted to the Digital Twin, enabling it to reflect the current state of the system.
- Control and Automation: PLCs can execute control algorithms that adjust the operation of machinery, motors, and other components based on real-time data. For instance, in a power grid Digital Twin, PLCs can automate processes like switching, fault detection, and load balancing.
- Communication with Digital Twins: PLCs communicate with Digital Twins by transmitting data via standard communication protocols such as Modbus, OPC UA, or MQTT. This enables the real-time synchronization of the physical system and the digital model.
- Edge Computing: PLCs often feature edge computing capabilities, allowing them to process data locally before sending it to higher-level systems or the cloud. This helps in reducing latency and improving the response time for real-time applications.

Applications in Digital Twin:

- Industrial Automation: PLCs are widely used in manufacturing and process automation. Digital Twins of manufacturing plants can utilize data from PLCs to simulate, monitor, and optimize production processes in real-time.
- Energy Systems: In electrical power systems, PLCs can control and monitor substations, transformers, and circuit breakers, providing data for the Digital Twin to simulate grid behavior, predict faults, and optimize load distribution.

Supervisory Control and Data Acquisition (SCADA)
SCADA (Supervisory Control and Data Acquisition) systems are used to monitor and control industrial processes, infrastructure,

and facility operations. SCADA systems typically operate over large geographic areas, including power plants, water treatment facilities, and manufacturing plants. They collect data from various sensors, relay it to central monitoring systems, and allow operators to remotely control equipment and respond to system events.

SCADA systems are integral in connecting the Digital Twin to the physical world, as they provide the infrastructure to acquire data from sensors, execute control commands, and provide visibility into system performance. SCADA systems are designed for large-scale, distributed systems, making them particularly useful in Digital Twin applications for grid management, energy distribution, and facility monitoring.

Key Features and Functions:

- Real-Time Data Monitoring: SCADA systems gather real-time data from sensors and field devices, such as temperature sensors, voltage sensors, and flow meters. This data is sent to the central control station or cloud-based Digital Twin for analysis.
- Remote Control: Operators can use SCADA systems to remotely control machinery and equipment. In the context of a Digital Twin, operators can make real-time adjustments based on insights provided by the virtual model, such as adjusting the output of power plants or switching energy sources in a smart grid.
- Alarms and Notifications: SCADA systems are equipped with alarm mechanisms that notify operators of abnormal conditions, such as equipment malfunctions or safety hazards. These alarms can trigger actions in the Digital Twin, such as predictive maintenance notifications or automatic control adjustments.
- Historical Data Logging and Analysis: SCADA systems store historical data for later analysis, enabling operators and engineers to perform diagnostics, trend analysis, and long-term optimization of systems. This historical data can also be used to refine the Digital Twin model over time.

Applications in Digital Twin:

- Smart Grids: SCADA systems are crucial in managing the distribution of electricity in smart grids. By integrating SCADA with Digital Twin technology, operators can simulate and predict the behavior of the grid, ensuring reliability and minimizing disruptions.
- Oil and Gas: SCADA systems are widely used in the oil and gas industry for pipeline monitoring, wellhead control, and refinery operations. Digital Twins in this sector can leverage SCADA data to optimize extraction processes and monitor equipment health in real-time.

Embedded Systems

Embedded systems are specialized computing systems designed to perform specific control functions within larger mechanical or electrical systems. These systems typically consist of a microcontroller or microprocessor, memory, input/output interfaces, and software that interact with sensors, actuators, and other hardware components. Embedded systems are used in a wide range of applications, including industrial automation, robotics, automotive, and consumer electronics.

In the context of Digital Twins, embedded systems provide the crucial hardware infrastructure for monitoring and controlling physical assets in real-time. They often operate at the edge of the network, gathering data directly from sensors and making local decisions before transmitting the data to higher-level control systems or Digital Twins.

Key Features and Functions:

- Sensor Integration: Embedded systems interface with sensors to collect data from physical processes. These sensors could monitor various parameters, such as temperature, pressure, humidity, and vibration, all of which are vital for creating an accurate Digital Twin model.

- Real-Time Control: Embedded systems can execute real-time control algorithms, which allow them to respond to sensor data instantaneously. This capability is crucial for applications such as motor control, process regulation, and fault detection, where swift responses are required.
- Edge Processing: Many embedded systems feature edge computing capabilities, processing data locally and reducing the need for constant communication with central systems. This allows for faster decision-making and reduces the strain on communication networks.
- Communication Protocols: Embedded systems often support communication protocols such as Modbus, CAN bus, and MQTT, allowing them to exchange data with other systems, including Digital Twins. They can act as nodes within a larger network, providing real-time insights to the Digital Twin model.

Applications in Digital Twin:

- Industrial IoT (IIoT): Embedded systems are often used in IIoT applications, where they monitor and control industrial machinery and equipment. By collecting data from sensors and executing control commands, they provide the Digital Twin with real-time information that can be used for predictive maintenance, performance optimization, and fault detection.
- Automated Vehicles: In the automotive industry, embedded systems are used to control vehicle components such as motors, brakes, and steering. A Digital Twin of an autonomous vehicle can integrate data from embedded systems to simulate the vehicle's behavior in real-time, ensuring safe and efficient operation.

Hardware platforms such as PLCs, SCADA systems, and embedded systems are integral to the success of Digital Twin technology, providing the necessary interfaces for data acquisition, real-time control, and system monitoring. These platforms enable the synchronization of the physical and digital worlds, ensuring that the virtual model accurately reflects the current state of the system. By integrating real-time data and executing control commands, hardware platforms play a pivotal role in improving system performance, reducing operational risks, and enhancing the overall reliability of Digital Twin applications across industries like electrical engineering, manufacturing, and transportation. As the field of Digital Twins continues to evolve, these hardware platforms will remain at the core of enabling more intelligent, autonomous, and optimized systems.

CLOUD AND EDGE COMPUTING PLATFORMS

Cloud and Edge Computing platforms are pivotal in the implementation and scalability of Digital Twin (DT) systems. They enable the efficient collection, processing, analysis, and storage of massive volumes of data generated by real-world systems and devices. These computing paradigms support the real-time operation, remote accessibility, and intelligent decision-making capabilities of Digital Twins—making them foundational technologies in sectors such as electrical engineering, manufacturing, energy, healthcare, and smart cities.

This section provides an in-depth exploration of both Cloud Computing and Edge Computing, their roles in Digital Twin architectures, and how they complement each other to create scalable, reliable, and responsive digital systems.

Cloud Computing Platforms

Cloud computing involves delivering computing services—such as servers, storage, databases, networking, software, and analytics—over the internet ("the cloud"). In the context of Digital Twins, cloud platforms offer a centralized environment where data can be stored, processed, and analyzed using powerful computing resources. Leading cloud providers such as Amazon Web Services (AWS), Microsoft Azure, and Google Cloud Platform (GCP) offer services tailored for IoT, AI, and Digital Twin applications.

Key Functions in Digital Twins:

Centralized Data Storage and Management: Cloud platforms provide vast storage capabilities to manage data from various sources such as sensors, devices, and control systems. They support structured and unstructured data, including time-series sensor data, logs, images, and simulations.

Scalability: Cloud platforms can scale resources up or down dynamically based on the demands of the Digital Twin system. For example, as more IoT devices are added to a smart grid or factory floor, the cloud infrastructure can handle the increased data without performance degradation.

Advanced Analytics and AI: Cloud computing provides access to high-performance AI/ML tools and big data analytics engines. These tools enable Digital Twins to perform predictive maintenance, anomaly detection, and optimization by analyzing historical and real-time data.

Simulation and Modeling: Cloud platforms support simulation tools that can run complex models and what-if scenarios. Engineers and researchers can test different operational strategies in a safe digital environment before applying them to the physical system.

Integration and Interoperability: Cloud services offer APIs and SDKs to integrate Digital Twin platforms with other enterprise systems such as ERP, MES, and CRM. This promotes seamless workflow automation and data-driven decision-making across the organization.

Remote Monitoring and Control: Cloud computing enables remote access to Digital Twin dashboards and control interfaces from anywhere in the world. This is especially important for managing infrastructure in remote or hazardous environments.

Applications:

- Smart grids: Managing and optimizing power distribution networks.
- Industrial automation: Monitoring factory processes and optimizing production.

- Smart buildings: Managing energy efficiency and HVAC systems remotely.
- Renewable energy: Centralized monitoring of solar farms and wind turbines.

Edge Computing Platforms

Edge computing refers to the practice of processing data closer to the location where it is generated, such as near sensors or embedded devices. This is particularly useful for Digital Twins that require ultra-low latency, high reliability, and real-time responsiveness. Unlike cloud computing, which centralizes data in distant data centers, edge computing enables data processing at or near the source of data generation.

Key Functions in Digital Twins:

- Real-Time Data Processing: Edge devices can process sensor data immediately upon collection, making them ideal for applications where latency must be minimized. For example, in power electronics or autonomous systems, split-second decisions based on local data can be critical.
- Reduced Bandwidth Requirements: By processing data locally, edge computing reduces the amount of data that needs to be transmitted to the cloud. Only relevant or pre-processed data is sent, which conserves bandwidth and reduces costs.
- Improved Reliability: Edge devices can continue to function even when the internet connection is unstable or unavailable. This ensures that the Digital Twin remains operational during connectivity issues, a crucial factor in mission-critical environments.
- Enhanced Security and Privacy: Sensitive data can be processed and stored locally at the edge, reducing the risk of data breaches or compliance issues associated with transferring data to cloud servers.
- Localized Control: Edge platforms can run control algorithms and actuate devices in real time. This is especially useful in

industrial automation and electric drive systems, where speed and reliability are paramount.

Examples of Edge Platforms and Devices:

- IoT Gateways: Act as intermediaries between IoT sensors and the cloud, offering local processing.
- Edge Servers: High-performance systems placed near the data source to run analytics and AI models.
- Microcontrollers and Single-Board Computers: Devices like Raspberry Pi and Arduino used for localized control in small-scale systems.
- Edge AI Chips: Specialized hardware such as NVIDIA Jetson or Intel Movidius for AI inference at the edge.

Applications:

- Smart factories: Controlling machines and robots with minimal latency.
- Energy systems: Real-time monitoring and fault detection in transformers and substations.
- Smart transportation: Managing traffic signals and autonomous vehicles in real-time.
- Building automation: Instant control of lighting, HVAC, and security systems.

Cloud-Edge Synergy

A modern Digital Twin architecture often leverages a hybrid approach that combines both cloud and edge computing to take advantage of the strengths of each. This integration ensures a balanced distribution of workloads, enabling efficient real-time control and global-scale data analysis.

How They Work Together:

- Edge handles immediate, time-sensitive tasks such as data acquisition, device control, and real-time alerts.
- Cloud handles long-term storage, global analytics, model training, historical trend analysis, and remote access.

For example, in a wind farm application, edge devices near turbines can detect anomalies and shut down equipment in milliseconds, while the cloud analyzes long-term wind patterns and recommends maintenance schedules.

Benefits of Integration:

- High availability and resilience.
- Optimized resource usage.
- Reduced network congestion.
- Improved decision-making based on both real-time and historical insights.

Cloud and Edge Computing platforms are foundational to the effective implementation of Digital Twin systems. While cloud computing provides the power of centralized analytics, scalability, and remote management, edge computing ensures that Digital Twins can respond quickly and reliably to real-world events. Together, they enable a robust and flexible infrastructure that supports the full lifecycle of Digital Twins—from data acquisition and real-time control to predictive analytics and decision-making. As the adoption of Digital Twins continues to grow across industries, the role of these computing platforms will become even more critical in building intelligent, connected, and autonomous systems.

DATA ANALYTICS AND VISUALIZATION TOOLS

Data analytics and visualization tools are essential components of Digital Twin architectures. These tools are responsible for transforming raw data collected from physical assets into meaningful insights and actionable intelligence. In a Digital Twin environment, the value lies not only in replicating the physical system digitally but also in understanding its behavior, predicting future states, and optimizing performance through data-driven decision-making. Data analytics and visualization act as the cognitive interface between humans and the complex data ecosystems of Digital Twins.

Importance of Data Analytics in Digital Twins

Digital Twins are built on continuous streams of real-time data from sensors, IoT devices, and external systems. The role of data analytics is to process and analyze this data to enable a deeper understanding of system conditions, identify anomalies, uncover hidden patterns, and drive decision-making.

Key Functions of Data Analytics in Digital Twins:

Descriptive Analytics

This form of analytics answers the question "What happened?" by summarizing historical data. It involves monitoring real-time metrics such as voltage, current, temperature, or speed in electrical systems and presenting this information through dashboards and reports.

Diagnostic Analytics

Diagnostic analytics digs deeper to answer "Why did it happen?" by identifying root causes of failures, disturbances, or inefficiencies. For example, if a transformer overheats, analytics can trace it back to overloading or environmental conditions.

Predictive Analytics

Predictive models use historical and real-time data to forecast future events. In Digital Twins, this may involve predicting when a machine component will fail or estimating future load demands in an electrical grid.

Prescriptive Analytics

This advanced form of analytics goes beyond prediction by recommending specific actions to achieve desired outcomes. It helps in optimizing performance, reducing costs, and improving safety, such as recommending maintenance schedules or optimal routing in a distribution system.

Real-Time Stream Analytics

This involves processing data as it is received, enabling instantaneous decision-making. Critical in power systems and automation, real-time analytics allow for quick fault detection, automatic load balancing, or voltage regulation.

Visualization Tools in Digital Twins

While analytics provide insights, visualization tools convert these insights into easily interpretable graphical formats. Effective visualization is crucial for engineers, operators, and decision-makers to monitor system performance, diagnose problems, and simulate scenarios.

Key Visualization Features in Digital Twins:

Dashboards and Control Panels

Interactive dashboards display real-time data, KPIs (Key Performance Indicators), alerts, and trends. Users can customize views to focus on specific metrics like energy consumption, system temperature, or fault occurrences.

3D Visualization and Augmented Reality (AR)

Digital Twins often include 3D models that replicate the structure and operation of the physical system. Combined with AR, users can visualize internal system components and performance layers in real space, which is useful for maintenance and training.

Heat Maps and Graphs

Heat maps visually represent parameter intensities (like heat or vibration) across a system, helping identify stress points. Graphs show trends over time, correlations, and patterns in parameters like voltage variation or mechanical wear.

Geospatial Visualization

For applications like smart grids and renewable energy farms, geospatial tools show the status and health of distributed assets on maps, helping to manage geographically dispersed resources effectively.

Scenario Simulations

Visual simulations allow engineers to model and visualize "what-if" scenarios—e.g., how a fault in one substation impacts the rest of the grid. This helps in risk assessment and planning.

Tools and Platforms for Data Analytics and Visualization

A variety of commercial and open-source tools are available for integrating analytics and visualization in Digital Twins.

Popular Analytics Tools:

- Python and R – Languages with powerful libraries (e.g., Pandas, Scikit-learn, TensorFlow) for data analysis and machine learning.
- MATLAB/Simulink – Widely used in engineering for simulation and advanced signal processing.
- Apache Spark and Hadoop – Big data platforms for large-scale data processing.

Visualization Tools and Platforms:

- Power BI and Tableau – Business intelligence tools for creating interactive dashboards and visual reports.
- Grafana – Open-source platform ideal for real-time monitoring with IoT integration.
- Unity/Unreal Engine – Used for creating immersive 3D visualizations in industrial applications.
- ThingWorx, Siemens Mindsphere, and GE Predix – Industrial-grade platforms that combine Digital Twin modeling, analytics, and visualization in one ecosystem.

Applications in Electrical Engineering

In the context of electrical systems, data analytics and visualization play a critical role in:

- Condition Monitoring: Identifying issues in transformers, motors, and switchgear based on vibration, temperature, or electrical signatures.
- Energy Management: Analyzing consumption patterns to reduce waste and improve efficiency.

- Grid Stability: Visualizing voltage fluctuations and frequency stability across distributed systems.
- Predictive Maintenance: Forecasting failures of circuit breakers, inverters, or batteries to schedule repairs and avoid downtime.
- Power Quality Analysis: Detecting harmonics, voltage dips, and transients through real-time analytics.

Benefits and Challenges
Benefits:

- Enhanced decision-making through actionable insights.
- Reduced downtime via predictive maintenance.
- Improved system performance and reliability.
- Greater situational awareness with intuitive visual interfaces.

Challenges:

- Managing and integrating data from diverse sources.
- Ensuring data quality and consistency.
- Handling high volumes of real-time data (data velocity and volume).
- Designing user-friendly and meaningful visualizations.

Data analytics and visualization tools are indispensable to unlocking the full potential of Digital Twins. They enable users to interpret complex system data, detect trends, predict failures, and optimize operations. As the Digital Twin ecosystem evolves with more IoT devices, AI integration, and higher data granularity, the role of sophisticated analytics and visualization will become even more critical. Future developments will likely include more intuitive visual interfaces, integration with virtual and augmented reality, and AI-powered analytics engines that provide autonomous decision support in real-time.

EIGHT

IMPLEMENTATION STRATEGIES

Implementing Digital Twin technology in electrical engineering systems requires a structured and strategic approach that bridges the gap between theoretical models and practical, real-world deployment. While the concept of Digital Twins offers transformative benefits—such as real-time system monitoring, predictive maintenance, operational optimization, and improved lifecycle management—realizing these benefits depends heavily on effective implementation strategies. These strategies encompass multiple dimensions: from technical infrastructure and data integration, to cross-functional collaboration, process reengineering, and change management.

A successful implementation begins with a clear understanding of the organizational objectives and system requirements, followed by careful planning of architecture, technologies, and tools that align with these goals. This includes identifying the specific assets to be digitized, selecting appropriate data acquisition methods, determining communication protocols, and integrating analytics and visualization layers. Furthermore, strategic implementation involves selecting suitable platforms—whether on-premises, cloud, or edge-based—and ensuring seamless interoperability between existing systems like SCADA, PLCs, and ERP solutions.

Another critical aspect of implementation is stakeholder involvement. Engineers, IT teams, data scientists, and operational managers must work together to co-design a scalable and robust system that reflects the dynamic nature of physical operations. Simultaneously, cybersecurity frameworks must be built into the design to protect sensitive infrastructure data. Pilot projects and proof-of-concept models often serve as stepping stones, allowing organizations to experiment with Digital Twin solutions in a controlled environment before full-scale deployment.

Over the course of five pages, this section will explore in detail the step-by-step process of implementing Digital Twins—from planning and technology selection to deployment, testing, and maintenance. It will also cover the challenges organizations face, such as integration with legacy systems, data governance issues, and the need for skilled personnel. Moreover, best practices, case studies, and emerging trends in implementation (like agile development, model-based systems engineering, and AI-assisted twins) will be discussed to provide a comprehensive understanding of how to turn the vision of Digital Twins into operational reality in the electrical engineering domain.

NINE

LIFECYCLE OF A DIGITAL TWINS

The lifecycle of a Digital Twin in electrical systems refers to the series of phases it undergoes from initial conception to retirement. Much like the physical systems it mirrors, a Digital Twin evolves over time, adapting to new requirements, environmental changes, and technological advancements. Understanding the lifecycle is crucial for successfully planning, deploying, and maintaining a Digital Twin to ensure it delivers continuous value throughout the lifespan of the corresponding physical asset or system.

Conceptualization and Design

The lifecycle begins with defining the goals and scope of the Digital Twin. This phase involves identifying which electrical systems or components will be digitally twinned, what data needs to be collected, and what outcomes are expected—such as performance monitoring, predictive maintenance, or system optimization. Design decisions are made regarding the model architecture, simulation fidelity, sensor placement, data types (voltage, current, temperature, etc.), and integration points with existing control and IT systems.

Key Activities:

- Defining objectives (e.g., monitoring transformers, optimizing power flows).
- Mapping the physical system and identifying critical parameters.
- Selecting modeling techniques (physics-based, data-driven, or hybrid).
- Planning for interoperability with existing systems (SCADA, PLCs).

Data Acquisition and Model Development

After the design stage, the next step is collecting real-time and historical data to build and calibrate the digital model. Sensors and IoT devices installed on the physical electrical systems capture data such as voltage levels, current flows, frequency deviations, temperature, power factor, and harmonics. This data is used to create a dynamic digital representation that reflects the real-time state and behavior of the system.

- Installing sensors and data acquisition units.
- Streaming and storing real-time operational data.
- Developing and refining simulation models.
- Validating model accuracy with test cases.

Integration and Commissioning

Once the model is developed, it must be integrated into the broader digital ecosystem. This includes establishing communication protocols, connecting to databases, cloud platforms, and visualization tools. The Digital Twin is tested in a simulated environment to ensure it can respond correctly to various scenarios before being fully commissioned.

- Connecting the Digital Twin to live data streams.
- Testing functionality and system responses.
- Validating security and communication standards.
- Ensuring compatibility with control systems and dashboards.

Operation and Monitoring

This is the most active phase of the lifecycle, where the Digital Twin performs continuous monitoring and analysis of the electrical system in real time. It compares predicted behaviors with actual performance, detects anomalies, and provides insights for decision-making. Advanced Digital Twins use AI to automate responses, suggest maintenance actions, and optimize operations.

- Real-time monitoring of system health and performance.
- Generating alerts and insights for predictive maintenance.
- Automatically adjusting system parameters based on real-time data.
- Feeding operational data back into the model to improve accuracy.

Maintenance and Evolution

Over time, electrical systems may undergo physical changes such as upgrades, component replacements, or reconfiguration. The Digital Twin must be updated to reflect these changes to maintain its accuracy and reliability. This phase ensures the twin remains synchronized with the physical system and incorporates new learnings from ongoing data analysis.

- Updating model parameters and algorithms as systems evolve.
- Re-calibrating simulations after physical changes.
- Enhancing the Digital Twin with new features (e.g., AI modules).
- Incorporating feedback loops for continuous improvement.

Retirement or Repurposing

Eventually, the physical system may reach the end of its life cycle. At this stage, the Digital Twin can be decommissioned, archived for future reference, or repurposed to support the design of new systems. The historical data and performance analytics captured during the twin's life can provide invaluable insights for system planning, failure analysis, and lifecycle costing in future projects.

- Archiving Digital Twin models and data logs.
- Performing post-mortem analysis for performance review.
- Using learnings to inform the design of next-generation systems.
- Retiring outdated models or adapting them for new applications.

The lifecycle of a Digital Twin in electrical systems mirrors the journey of the physical system it represents—from design and deployment to optimization and eventual decommissioning. Each phase is interconnected and critical to maintaining the fidelity and functionality of the twin. By managing this lifecycle strategically, engineers and organizations can ensure that the Digital Twin delivers continuous value, supports efficient system operation, enhances decision-making, and contributes to a sustainable and intelligent energy infrastructure. As technologies advance, the lifecycle itself becomes more intelligent and autonomous, paving the way for self-updating, self-healing, and self-optimizing Digital Twins.

DATA MANAGEMENT AND REAL-TIME MONITORING

Data management and real-time monitoring are core components of an effective Digital Twin framework in electrical systems. These two functions work hand-in-hand to ensure that the digital representation of the physical asset remains accurate, responsive, and valuable throughout its operational lifecycle. In electrical engineering, where timing, accuracy, and system stability are critical, robust data handling and live system observation are indispensable.

Importance of Data in Digital Twin Systems

At the heart of every Digital Twin lies data—collected from sensors, meters, control systems, and operational software. This data includes electrical parameters such as voltage, current, frequency, power factor, harmonics, energy consumption, temperature, and environmental factors. Data not only feeds the digital model with real-time inputs but also serves to validate, calibrate, and optimize it.

- Monitoring the state of electrical components (transformers, breakers, cables, etc.).
- Predicting failures through pattern recognition and anomaly detection.
- Simulating "what-if" scenarios based on real system behavior.
- Making informed, data-driven decisions for operational control and maintenance planning.

Data Management Framework

Data management refers to how this massive influx of information is collected, stored, organized, processed, and accessed. Without proper data management, the accuracy and effectiveness of the Digital Twin can quickly degrade.

a. Data Collection and Ingestion

Sensors and IoT devices installed on electrical infrastructure continuously collect data. This data may come from:

- Smart meters
- Power quality analyzers
- Protection relays
- Supervisory Control and Data Acquisition (SCADA) systems
- Programmable Logic Controllers (PLCs)

Collected data is ingested through edge devices or gateways that pre-process and format it for further transmission.

b. Data Storage

Storage solutions depend on the volume, speed, and type of data. Some common methods include:

- Relational databases for structured historical data
- Time-series databases for high-frequency sensor data
- Cloud storage for scalability and remote access
- Edge storage for local processing and fast response

Proper storage ensures quick retrieval and supports analytics, machine learning, and historical tracking.

c. Data Preprocessing and Cleansing

Before analysis, raw data must be filtered to remove noise, outliers, or corrupt entries. Cleansing enhances data quality and improves the reliability of predictions and insights generated by the Digital Twin.

d. Data Governance and Security

Data must be protected to prevent tampering, loss, or unauthorized access. Governance policies manage:

- Data access rights and encryption
- Compliance with regulations (e.g., GDPR, NERC)
- Audit trails for traceability
- Backup and disaster recovery strategies

Real-Time Monitoring

Real-time monitoring enables the Digital Twin to mirror the current state of the physical system with high fidelity. This involves collecting and displaying live data as it happens, allowing engineers to make proactive decisions.

a. Real-Time Data Visualization

Dashboards display key performance indicators (KPIs) such as load levels, frequency deviations, voltage sags/swells, and energy flows. Visual representations may include:

- Digital mimic panels of substations
- Interactive 3D models of switchgear
- Heatmaps showing energy consumption
- Trend graphs and event timelines

b. Alerts and Event Detection

Monitoring systems can detect anomalies and trigger alarms in case of:

- Overloads or under-voltage conditions
- Equipment overheating
- Communication failures
- Unauthorized access attempts

Automated alerts can be sent via SMS, email, or through SCADA interfaces for immediate attention.

c. Predictive and Prescriptive Monitoring

With AI and machine learning, real-time monitoring becomes predictive. Instead of reacting to faults, the system can anticipate issues:

- Transformer failure prediction based on thermal and electrical stress
- Cable insulation deterioration through partial discharge patterns
- Load forecasting for balancing and switching decisions

Prescriptive analytics go one step further by recommending corrective actions or automatically initiating control strategies.

Integration with Control Systems

Real-time monitoring is tightly integrated with control systems like SCADA, DCS (Distributed Control Systems), and EMS (Energy Management Systems). This integration ensures:

- Immediate corrective action when thresholds are breached
- Automated load shedding or switching operations
- Adaptive protection settings based on system state

This closed-loop feedback system makes Digital Twins active participants in system control rather than passive observers.

Scalability and Performance

As the number of monitored devices grows, the data volume and frequency increase significantly. Efficient data pipelines, high-speed networks (like 5G), and edge computing are used to maintain low latency and high performance.

Performance considerations include:

- Latency minimization for time-critical actions
- Horizontal scaling of cloud resources
- Load balancing between edge and cloud processing
- Bandwidth optimization using data compression techniques

Benefits of Effective Data Management and Monitoring

- Enhanced reliability: Prevent failures before they occur through predictive monitoring.
- Operational efficiency: Optimize energy usage and resource allocation in real-time.
- Safety improvement: Detect faults or hazardous conditions instantly.
- Cost savings: Reduce downtime, maintenance costs, and energy waste.
- Informed decision-making: Use historical and live data to support planning and upgrades.

Data management and real-time monitoring form the backbone of any successful Digital Twin deployment in electrical systems. Together, they ensure that the digital counterpart remains an accurate, responsive, and intelligent reflection of the physical system. With advancements in sensor technology, high-speed data networks, cloud computing, and artificial intelligence, organizations can now manage vast data streams and monitor operations in real-time with unprecedented precision. This capability not only enhances operational control and system health but also lays the foundation for autonomous grid management, smart infrastructure, and next-generation energy solutions.

MODEL VALIDATION AND VERIFICATION

Model validation and verification (V&V) are critical processes in the development and implementation of Digital Twins, particularly in complex fields such as electrical systems. These steps ensure that the digital model accurately represents the physical system and behaves as expected under all relevant conditions. Without proper V&V, the insights and decisions driven by the Digital Twin could be flawed, potentially leading to system inefficiencies, malfunctions, or even failures.

Understanding Model Verification and Validation

Although they are often mentioned together, verification and validation serve distinct purposes:

- Verification: "Are we building the model right?"

This process checks that the Digital Twin model is correctly implemented based on the design specifications. It involves examining the model for coding errors, logical consistency, mathematical accuracy, and the correct application of algorithms.

- Validation: "Are we building the right model?"

Validation ensures that the model accurately represents the real-world system it is meant to simulate. It compares model behavior with actual system data to confirm that predictions and responses match reality.

Both processes are essential for building trust in the Digital Twin and ensuring it can be used for operational, planning, and diagnostic purposes in electrical engineering applications.

Steps in Model Verification

Verification involves a range of technical and analytical tasks:

a. Code and Algorithm Review

Engineers and developers conduct reviews to ensure that:

- Mathematical equations are implemented correctly.
- Algorithms for system behavior (like voltage/current dynamics) are stable and logical.
- No syntax or logic errors exist in the codebase.

b. Software Testing
Testing is conducted through:

- Unit testing: Each module (e.g., transformer model, load flow calculator) is tested individually.
- Integration testing: Interconnected components (e.g., switchgear with protection systems) are tested together to ensure compatibility.
- Regression testing: Ensures that updates do not break existing functionalities.

c. Simulation Consistency
The model is simulated under standard operating conditions and edge cases to ensure:

- Numerical stability (no erratic outputs).
- Time-step accuracy for dynamic simulations.
- Consistent results across repeated simulations.

Steps in Model Validation
Validation focuses on aligning the model with the real-world electrical system. It includes:
a. Data Collection from Physical Systems
Actual data from sensors, SCADA systems, and operational logs is collected. This data includes:

- Voltage, current, frequency, and power data.
- Protection relay events and switching operations.
- Thermal measurements and environmental factors.

b. Model Calibration
Parameters in the model (e.g., resistance, reactance, capacitance, load profiles) are adjusted so that the model output aligns with real-world measurements. Calibration ensures the Digital Twin accurately reflects the behavior of the physical system under

normal and abnormal conditions.

c. Comparative Analysis

The model's outputs are compared with real-world results under identical conditions:

- Simulated vs. measured voltages at different nodes.
- Load flow predictions vs. actual power distribution.
- Response to faults, switching, or load variations.

Statistical tools like Root Mean Square Error (RMSE), Mean Absolute Percentage Error (MAPE), and correlation coefficients are often used to quantify the alignment.

Techniques and Tools for V&V

Various techniques and software tools support the V&V process:

- Hardware-in-the-Loop (HIL) Simulation: Physical hardware (e.g., protection relays or inverters) is tested with the digital model in real time to validate behavior under live conditions.
- Scenario Testing: The model is subjected to fault conditions, peak loads, renewable variability, etc., to test its response.
- AI/ML-based Validation: Machine learning algorithms can detect anomalies between expected and actual data, improving validation speed and accuracy.
- Digital Simulation Platforms: Tools like MATLAB/Simulink, PSCAD, PSS®E, and DIgSILENT PowerFactory offer built-in environments for testing and validating electrical models.

Challenges in Model Validation and Verification

Data Inconsistency

Poor-quality, incomplete, or outdated data can hinder validation. Synchronization between time-stamped data and model simulations is essential.

Model Complexity

Electrical systems are dynamic and complex, especially with integration of renewables and smart grids. Creating a fully accurate model of all interactions can be difficult and may require simplifications.

Changing System Conditions

Real-world systems evolve over time. New equipment, load changes, or control settings may require frequent re-validation of the model to maintain accuracy.

Computational Requirements

High-fidelity simulations with detailed components can be computationally intensive, especially during iterative validation cycles.

Best Practices for Effective V&V

- Use Modular Models: Break the model into subsystems for easier testing and calibration.
- Automate Testing: Use automated scripts to repeatedly test models against datasets.
- Maintain Version Control: Keep records of model versions and changes to trace discrepancies.
- Establish a Feedback Loop: Continuously collect new data from the physical system to revalidate and update the model.

Benefits of Rigorous Validation and Verification

- Accuracy: Ensures that decisions based on the Digital Twin are trustworthy.
- Reliability: Reduces risk of misoperations or incorrect fault diagnosis.
- Efficiency: Validated models improve simulation speed and confidence in optimization tasks.
- Regulatory Compliance: Helps meet industry standards and safety regulations for electrical systems.

Model validation and verification are foundational to the integrity and success of Digital Twin implementations in electrical engineering. While verification ensures the model is built correctly, validation ensures that it represents the physical reality with high fidelity. Together, these processes help ensure the Digital Twin can support real-time monitoring, predictive analytics, and autonomous decision-making with precision. In a domain where system reliability, safety, and performance are paramount, rigorous V&V practices provide the assurance needed to integrate Digital Twins into mission-critical electrical infrastructure.

CHALLENGES IN INTEGRATION AND DEPLOYMENT

The integration and deployment of Digital Twins in electrical systems offer transformative potential but are also accompanied by a range of significant challenges. These hurdles span technical, operational, financial, and organizational domains, and they must be carefully navigated to realize the full benefits of Digital Twin technology. From managing complex data streams and legacy systems to ensuring cybersecurity and aligning stakeholders, each phase of integration and deployment presents unique difficulties. Below is a detailed breakdown of the key challenges and considerations:

Complexity of System Integration

Electrical systems are composed of numerous subsystems—generation, transmission, distribution, protection, and control—each with its own standards, communication protocols, and hardware interfaces.

- Heterogeneity: Integrating data and operations from diverse devices such as transformers, circuit breakers, inverters, and sensors, each from different vendors, is technically demanding.
- Legacy Systems: Older infrastructure may not support modern communication standards or data formats, making integration with digital models difficult.
- Data Silos: In many utilities or industrial plants, data exists in disconnected systems, preventing seamless data exchange required for an integrated Digital Twin.

Solution Approaches:

- Adoption of middleware or standardized APIs for interoperability.
- Gradual modernization of legacy components or the use of digital retrofitting techniques.

Data Management and Quality

The reliability of a Digital Twin is directly tied to the quality, accuracy, and timeliness of its data inputs.

- Volume and Velocity: Electrical systems generate massive amounts of real-time data that must be ingested, processed, and stored efficiently.
- Inconsistent or Noisy Data: Sensor errors, data packet loss, or environmental interference can degrade data quality.
- Data Synchronization: Ensuring that all data is time-aligned for accurate simulation and analysis is a constant challenge.

Solution Approaches:

- Implement robust data cleansing, validation, and synchronization algorithms.
- Use edge computing to pre-process data and reduce network load

Cybersecurity and Privacy Concerns

Digital Twins are connected to critical infrastructure and collect sensitive operational data, making them attractive targets for cyberattacks.

- Attack Surfaces: The increased connectivity between IT (Information Technology) and OT (Operational Technology) systems introduces more entry points for malicious actors.
- Data Breaches and Tampering: Unauthorized access can lead to operational disruptions or compromise sensitive data like control strategies or grid topology.

Solution Approaches:

- Employ end-to-end encryption, secure authentication, and regular security audits.
- Adopt industry-standard frameworks like IEC 62443 for cybersecurity in industrial automation.

High Implementation Costs

Building a Digital Twin ecosystem requires significant initial investment in hardware, software, skilled personnel, and system design.

- Sensor Deployment and Network Infrastructure: Installing high-fidelity sensors and establishing reliable communication channels is expensive.
- Software Licensing and Customization: Proprietary platforms may require costly licenses and extensive customization for compatibility.
- Training and Skill Development: Teams must be trained in Digital Twin technology, simulation, analytics, and cybersecurity.

Solution Approaches:

- Conduct a cost-benefit analysis and start with pilot projects to demonstrate ROI.
- Consider open-source platforms or hybrid models to manage costs.

Real-Time Performance Requirements

Digital Twins in electrical systems must function in real-time or near real-time to provide actionable insights, especially for monitoring, fault diagnosis, and control.

- Latency Issues: Delays in data transmission or processing can lead to outdated or incorrect system representations.
- Computational Load: High-fidelity simulations and analytics can strain processing capabilities, especially when scaling across large systems.

Solution Approaches:

- Use distributed computing (e.g., edge-cloud hybrid architectures) to balance load and reduce latency.
- Optimize models for speed without sacrificing critical accuracy.

Scalability and Maintenance

As electrical systems grow, the Digital Twin must scale accordingly. However, maintaining consistency and accuracy across a scaled-up deployment is complex.

- Dynamic System Changes: Electrical systems are constantly evolving with new loads, distributed energy resources, and regulatory requirements.
- Model Drift: The digital model may become outdated as the physical system changes, requiring constant updates and validation.

Solution Approaches:

- Implement automated model update mechanisms using machine learning or real-time calibration techniques.
- Design modular and flexible architectures that can adapt to expansion.

Standardization and Interoperability

There is a lack of universal standards for building and operating Digital Twins across different sectors and equipment manufacturers.

- Vendor Lock-In: Proprietary tools and models may restrict flexibility or integration with other systems.
- Incompatibility: Disparate modeling standards or data formats create obstacles for seamless integration.

Solution Approaches:

- Promote the use of open standards like OPC UA, MQTT, and CIM (Common Information Model).
- Support industry initiatives for Digital Twin interoperability.

Organizational and Cultural Resistance

Introducing Digital Twins often requires a shift in how decisions are made and how systems are managed.

- Change Management: Staff may resist adopting new technologies due to fear of obsolescence or lack of understanding.
- Decision-Making Discrepancies: Traditional decision-makers may distrust automated or AI-based recommendations.

- Provide comprehensive training and involve end-users from early development stages.
- Demonstrate tangible benefits through pilot use cases and small-scale deployments.

Regulatory and Compliance Challenges

Utilities and electrical service providers operate under strict regulatory frameworks.

- Data Sovereignty and Compliance: Handling data, especially across borders, may involve legal restrictions.
- Safety and Certification: Systems must meet industry safety standards and certifications before deployment.

Solution Approaches:

- Engage with regulators early during planning and design phases.
- Ensure that systems and models are auditable and traceable.

While Digital Twins have the potential to revolutionize how electrical systems are monitored, controlled, and optimized, their integration and deployment are not without challenges. From the complexities of data management and cybersecurity to scalability, cost, and organizational readiness, a successful deployment demands a well-thought-out strategy that balances innovation with practicality. By identifying and addressing these barriers early, organizations can maximize the return on investment and pave the way for smarter, safer, and more resilient electrical infrastructure.

TEN

CASE STUDIES AND APPLICATIONS

The practical value of Digital Twin technology is most vividly illustrated through real-world case studies and applications across various sectors within electrical engineering. As a cutting-edge innovation, Digital Twins have transitioned from conceptual frameworks to impactful, operational tools that enhance system performance, reliability, and sustainability. Their versatility enables deployment in a wide array of electrical domains—ranging from smart grid optimization and fault detection in substations to predictive maintenance in power plants and integration of renewable energy sources. By creating a dynamic, real-time digital replica of physical electrical assets, Digital Twins empower engineers, operators, and decision-makers with unprecedented insight and control over their systems. These applications are not confined to theoretical or pilot environments; they are now being employed in full-scale utility networks, industrial automation systems, transportation infrastructures, and even rural electrification projects. The incorporation of case studies brings clarity to the conceptual benefits of Digital Twins, demonstrating their tangible outcomes such as reduced downtime, improved energy efficiency, lower maintenance costs, and enhanced grid resilience. Furthermore, these examples highlight the adaptability of Digital Twin frameworks to different geographical, technological, and organizational contexts, offering scalable and customizable solutions for diverse challenges. Through detailed exploration of these case studies, we not only understand the technical mechanisms of implementation but also gain insights into the strategic decisions, stakeholder involvement, and long-term impacts that shape successful Digital Twin deployments. Thus, this section serves as a bridge between theory and practice, showcasing how Digital Twin technology is driving innovation and transformation across the modern electrical engineering landscape.

REAL-WORLD USE CASES IN INDUSTRY

Digital Twin technology has rapidly transitioned from a futuristic concept to a transformative tool actively being used across various industrial sectors. Its adoption in the electrical engineering domain, in particular, is driven by the growing demand for intelligent systems that ensure operational efficiency, predictive maintenance, energy optimization, and reduced downtime. Real-world use cases showcase how Digital Twins are enabling industries to gain real-time visibility, simulate scenarios, and make data-driven decisions that improve performance and cut costs.

Smart Grid Optimization

One of the most prominent applications of Digital Twins is in the optimization of smart grids. Utilities across the globe use Digital Twins to monitor and simulate their electrical distribution networks. These digital models help predict load demands, detect anomalies, and optimize voltage and power flow in real time. For instance, the Italian utility company Enel has adopted Digital Twin technology to enhance its smart grid performance by simulating the effects of different grid configurations, analyzing load behavior, and improving fault response times.

- Improved fault detection and localization
- Real-time power flow analysis
- Energy loss reduction through grid optimization
- Better load balancing and peak shaving

Predictive Maintenance in Power Plants

Power generation facilities—whether thermal, nuclear, or renewable—are complex environments where unplanned outages can lead to significant financial losses. Digital Twins allow plant operators to create virtual replicas of turbines, generators, and control systems. These twins collect sensor data from physical assets and use AI algorithms to predict equipment degradation or failure. General Electric (GE) has successfully implemented Digital Twin solutions for its gas turbines, reducing maintenance costs and improving uptime through early anomaly detection.

- Reduced equipment downtime
- Extended asset life
- Predictive rather than reactive maintenance
- Lower operational and repair costs

Wind Farm Performance Monitoring

In the renewable energy sector, companies like Siemens Gamesa and Vestas use Digital Twins to monitor and control large-scale wind farms. Each wind turbine has a digital replica that provides insights into operational efficiency, blade health, and environmental conditions. These twins can simulate wear and tear, adjust turbine performance dynamically, and suggest proactive maintenance schedules, thereby increasing the energy output and reliability of the wind farm.

- Increased turbine efficiency
- Improved capacity factor of wind farms
- Real-time performance adjustments
- Reduction in manual inspections and downtime

Substation Automation and Reliability

Electric substations form the backbone of electricity transmission and distribution networks. Digital Twins in substations simulate all electrical components—such as transformers, breakers, relays, and switchgear—to provide real-time diagnostics, remote control, and predictive analytics. Companies like ABB and Schneider Electric use Digital Twins to create virtual control rooms, allowing operators to visualize electrical flows, anticipate overloads, and automate switching decisions.

- Enhanced system reliability
- Intelligent control and protection strategies
- Safer remote monitoring and control
- Real-time simulation of fault scenarios

Industrial Automation and Factory Energy Management

Digital Twins are also applied in industrial automation for factory energy management. Manufacturing plants use these digital models to simulate machine operation, monitor energy usage, and optimize production processes. For instance, Bosch uses Digital Twin solutions in its "Industry 4.0" facilities to track energy consumption of each machine, forecast energy demand, and adjust production schedules accordingly. This not only improves energy efficiency but also supports sustainability goals.

- Energy usage optimization
- Demand forecasting and load leveling
- Equipment health monitoring
- Waste and emission reduction

Electric Vehicle Charging Infrastructure

As electric vehicle (EV) adoption grows, utilities and municipalities are using Digital Twins to design and manage charging infrastructure. Digital models simulate the effects of EV charging on the local grid, helping operators determine optimal locations for chargers, evaluate power demands, and assess grid stability. Companies like Hitachi and Siemens are using Digital Twins in smart city projects to ensure efficient EV integration into urban power networks.

- Optimized charger placement
- Grid impact simulation
- Demand-side management
- Improved user experience through real-time data

Data Center Energy Optimization

Data centers are high-energy-consumption facilities. Companies like Google and Microsoft use Digital Twins to optimize data center cooling and power usage. By modeling airflow, temperature distribution, and server load, these twins help operators reduce cooling costs and improve power usage effectiveness (PUE). Real-time monitoring combined with predictive analytics enables autonomous adjustments for efficient operation.

- Reduced cooling costs
- Improved energy efficiency
- Predictive thermal management
- Enhanced operational sustainability

The real-world use cases of Digital Twin technology in industry reveal a significant shift toward intelligent, predictive, and automated systems. From power plants and substations to renewable energy and electric vehicle infrastructure, Digital Twins are helping industries achieve operational excellence, environmental sustainability, and economic efficiency. These applications not only validate the practical viability of Digital Twin systems but also pave the way for their broader adoption across other emerging sectors. As industries continue to digitize and adopt Industry 4.0 practices, the role of Digital Twins is expected to grow exponentially—fueling innovation and transforming the way electrical systems are monitored, managed, and maintained.

PREDICTIVE MAINTENANCE FOR ELECTRICAL ASSETS

Predictive Maintenance (PdM) represents a transformative strategy in the operation and upkeep of electrical assets, leveraging advanced technologies to forecast equipment failures before they occur. Unlike traditional maintenance approaches—such as reactive (fix after failure) or preventive (scheduled regardless of condition)—predictive maintenance focuses on the real-time condition and performance of assets. It uses a combination of sensor data, machine learning (ML), Artificial Intelligence (AI), Digital Twins, and analytics to monitor, assess, and predict the health of electrical components, thus allowing for timely, data-driven interventions.

Concept of Predictive Maintenance in Electrical Engineering

In electrical systems, assets like transformers, switchgear, circuit breakers, generators, motors, cables, inverters, and power electronic devices are critical for continuous and safe operation. Over time, these components experience wear and degradation due to thermal stress, electrical loading, mechanical fatigue, and environmental factors.

Predictive Maintenance aims to detect early signs of deterioration or failure through constant monitoring and predictive modeling. This enables engineers to plan maintenance at the optimal time—before a fault occurs, but without unnecessary downtime.

Technologies Enabling Predictive Maintenance

a. Sensors and IoT Devices

Modern electrical systems are equipped with sensors that collect data on:

- Voltage, current, and power quality
- Temperature and thermal imaging
- Vibration and mechanical movement
- Partial discharge and insulation resistance
- Oil levels and dissolved gas analysis (for transformers)

IoT (Internet of Things) devices connect these sensors to centralized monitoring platforms, enabling real-time data collection.

b. Digital Twins

Digital Twins replicate the physical behavior of electrical assets in a virtual environment. They simulate equipment performance under various conditions, allowing predictive models to test and forecast future outcomes.

Example: A Digital Twin of a power transformer can simulate thermal behavior under high loads and predict winding degradation based on past patterns and current trends.

c. Data Analytics and Machine Learning

Machine learning models analyze historical and real-time data to detect patterns, anomalies, and trends that may precede a failure. Common algorithms include:

- Regression analysis for estimating time to failure
- Classification models for fault diagnosis
- Neural networks for pattern recognition and anomaly detection

d. Cloud and Edge Computing

Cloud platforms offer vast storage and processing power to run predictive algorithms on large datasets. Edge computing allows for real-time analytics at the asset level, minimizing latency and ensuring faster response.

Key Applications in Electrical Assets
a. Transformers

- Monitoring oil quality, winding temperature, and partial discharges
- Predicting insulation failure or overload risk
- Extending asset life by scheduling maintenance based on degradation rate

b. Electric Motors and Drives

- Vibration and acoustic analysis for bearing faults
- Thermal profiling to detect overheating
- Torque and speed analysis to identify misalignment or wear

c. Circuit Breakers and Switchgear

- Contact wear and arc duration monitoring
- Predicting the need for lubrication, cleaning, or part replacement
- Reducing unplanned outages in substations

d. Power Electronic Devices (Inverters, Converters)

- Thermal cycling and voltage stress monitoring
- Failure prediction in semiconductor components
- Managing lifecycle of inverter components in renewable energy systems

Benefits of Predictive Maintenance

- **Reduced Downtime:** Avoids sudden failures, ensuring higher availability and reliability of electrical systems
- **Cost Savings:** Minimizes unnecessary preventive maintenance and reduces repair costs
- **Extended Asset Life:** Timely interventions slow down degradation and enhance longevity
- **Improved Safety:** Early detection of faults prevents catastrophic failures and hazards
- **Better Planning:** Maintenance activities can be scheduled alongside production needs and resource availability
- **Sustainability:** Reduces energy waste from malfunctioning equipment and lowers carbon footprint by improving efficiency

Challenges in Implementation

- Data Quality and Volume: Effective prediction relies on accurate, high-resolution, and continuous data
- Integration Complexity: Integrating predictive tools with legacy systems can be difficult
- Initial Costs: Sensor installations, software platforms, and training require upfront investment
- Model Accuracy: Machine learning models need time and data to become accurate and reliable
- Cybersecurity: IoT-connected maintenance systems must be protected from cyber threats

Industry Examples

- ABB uses predictive analytics on their electrical equipment like circuit breakers and relays to anticipate wear and optimize servicing intervals.
- Siemens applies AI-driven predictive maintenance in its gas-insulated switchgear and smart substations for utility companies.
- Schneider Electric deploys predictive services for power quality monitoring in commercial buildings and industrial plants.
- General Electric (GE) integrates Digital Twins and PdM in rotating electrical machines across thermal power plants.

Predictive Maintenance is revolutionizing the way electrical assets are managed. It enables a shift from reactive to proactive maintenance strategies, improving reliability, lowering costs, and enhancing asset performance. As Digital Twins, AI, IoT, and analytics mature and converge, predictive maintenance will become even more intelligent, autonomous, and essential to the sustainable digital future of electrical engineering systems.

OPTIMIZATION IN POWER DISTRIBUTION NETWORKS

Optimization in power distribution networks (PDNs) refers to the process of improving the performance, efficiency, and reliability of electrical power systems that distribute electricity from substations to end consumers. These networks consist of transformers, switches, circuit breakers, power lines, and loads, and the goal of optimization is to ensure that electrical power is delivered with the least loss, minimum downtime, and at the most efficient cost. As electrical grids become more complex, the integration of renewable energy sources, distributed energy resources (DERs), and smart technologies, optimization plays a vital role in balancing supply, demand, and resource utilization.

Key Objectives of Optimization in Power Distribution Networks

The optimization process aims to achieve several key objectives:

a. Minimizing Power Losses

Power losses in distribution networks primarily occur due to the resistance of conductors and other electrical components. Optimizing the network design, configuration, and operational parameters can minimize these losses, improving overall system efficiency. These losses can be categorized into:

- Technical Losses: Energy lost due to resistance in cables, transformers, and other network components.
- Non-Technical Losses: Losses attributed to energy theft, metering inaccuracies, or faults in data collection.

b. Enhancing Reliability

Reliability in power distribution refers to the ability of the network to consistently supply electricity without interruptions. Optimizing the configuration of the network ensures faster fault detection, minimal downtime, and efficient restoration of power during outages. This includes:

- Fault Detection and Isolation: Quick identification of faults and rapid isolation of affected sections.
- Restoration Strategies: Ensuring that power is restored efficiently after faults, using rerouting or backup power.

c. Load Balancing

Load balancing involves evenly distributing the electrical load across the network to avoid overloading certain parts of the grid. Proper load balancing ensures that power is used efficiently and that no single component, such as transformers or feeders, is subjected to excess load.

d. Cost Optimization

Cost optimization focuses on minimizing operational and maintenance costs. This includes optimizing the deployment and maintenance of infrastructure, reducing energy losses, and improving the use of renewable energy sources to reduce fuel costs in thermal power generation.

Techniques and Methods for Optimizing Power Distribution Networks

Several advanced techniques and strategies are used to achieve optimal performance in PDNs. These methods leverage various optimization algorithms, technologies, and models to enhance grid operation.

a. Network Reconfiguration

Network reconfiguration involves changing the topology of the distribution network by opening and closing switches. This can help in:

- Redistributing power in the network when one section is experiencing high demand or faults.
- Reducing power losses by ensuring that power flows along the most efficient paths.
- Improving voltage regulation by balancing the load across different parts of the network.

Network reconfiguration is a dynamic process, meaning it can be adjusted in real time based on changing conditions such as demand, generation, or fault events.

b. Voltage Optimization

Voltage optimization involves controlling the voltage levels at various points in the distribution network to minimize losses and improve efficiency. By adjusting the voltage set points, the distribution network can:

- Reduce the power losses in conductors and transformers.
- Improve the performance of electric motors and other equipment sensitive to voltage variations.
- Comply with regulatory standards for voltage levels, ensuring safe and reliable delivery of power.

c. Demand Response and Peak Shaving

Demand response (DR) is a strategy where consumers are encouraged (or incentivized) to reduce their electricity usage during peak demand periods. DR helps in reducing the load on the distribution network, particularly during high-demand events such as hot summer days or industrial spikes. The use of smart meters and real-time monitoring can provide consumers with real-time data to adjust their power usage.

Peak shaving involves shifting energy consumption to off-peak hours by leveraging storage solutions or adjusting operational schedules, which reduces the strain on the grid during high-demand periods.

d. Distributed Energy Resources (DER) Integration

Distributed Energy Resources, such as solar panels, wind turbines, energy storage systems, and small-scale generators, can be integrated into the power distribution network to optimize energy generation and consumption. The integration of DERs offers several benefits:

- **Local Generation:** Reduces reliance on centralized power plants and transmission lines, leading to reduced losses.
- **Energy Storage:** Batteries and other storage solutions can store excess renewable energy during periods of high generation and discharge it when demand is high or renewable output is low.

- **Renewable Integration:** Solar and wind power can be integrated into the grid, balancing demand and reducing dependency on fossil fuels.

The optimization of DERs involves managing their performance, ensuring smooth integration with the grid, and addressing challenges such as intermittency and variability.

e. Advanced Metering Infrastructure (AMI)

Advanced Metering Infrastructure provides real-time data on energy usage, voltage, current, and other parameters across the distribution network. This data can be analyzed to identify inefficiencies, detect faults early, and optimize the dispatch of power. AMI enables utilities to:

- Implement time-of-use pricing to encourage consumers to use electricity during off-peak times.
- Collect granular data for forecasting, which is essential for optimizing the load on the network.
- Improve customer satisfaction by providing accurate billing and real-time consumption data.

f. Artificial Intelligence and Machine Learning

AI and machine learning (ML) algorithms can be applied to optimize the operation and management of power distribution networks. These technologies use historical and real-time data to learn from past experiences, detect patterns, and predict future grid behaviors. Machine learning can:

- Forecast demand and adjust power dispatch accordingly.
- Predict and prevent faults before they occur.
- Optimize the operation of DERs and energy storage systems.
- Enhance decision-making in network reconfiguration and load balancing.

Challenges in Optimizing Power Distribution Networks

While there are significant benefits to optimizing PDNs, several challenges must be addressed:

a. Complexity of Modern Power Grids

As grids become more complex, with the integration of DERs, renewable energy, and smart technologies, optimization becomes more difficult. The increasing number of variables, such as fluctuating renewable generation, varying demand patterns, and diverse consumer behaviors, complicates the decision-making process for grid operators.

b. Data Management and Integration

Optimization requires access to large amounts of high-quality, real-time data. The challenge lies in integrating this data from various sources, including sensors, smart meters, SCADA systems, and other grid management tools, into a unified system that can be analyzed and acted upon effectively.

c. Cybersecurity Concerns

With the increased use of digital tools and communication technologies, power distribution networks become more vulnerable to cyber-attacks. Optimizing grid operations while maintaining the security and integrity of data and control systems is a major concern for utilities and operators.

d. Regulatory and Market Constraints

Regulatory frameworks and market rules can sometimes impede the full implementation of optimization strategies. Utilities must navigate a complex landscape of regulations, price controls, and market structures that may limit their ability to fully optimize network operations.

The Future of Optimization in Power Distribution Networks

As technology continues to evolve, the future of optimization in power distribution networks holds significant promise. Key trends include:

- Increased use of AI and machine learning to automate decision-making processes.

- Greater integration of renewable energy and distributed energy resources to balance supply and demand.
- Enhanced grid flexibility through dynamic network reconfiguration and real-time response capabilities.
- Advanced predictive analytics for anticipating network issues and preventing failures before they occur.

The convergence of technologies like AI, IoT, and big data analytics, along with regulatory support and increased investment in smart grid infrastructure, will pave the way for more efficient, resilient, and sustainable power distribution networks in the future.

Optimization in power distribution networks is a critical process to enhance the efficiency, reliability, and cost-effectiveness of electrical grids. With the integration of advanced technologies such as smart meters, renewable energy, AI, and machine learning, utilities can better manage demand, reduce losses, improve reliability, and support the integration of cleaner energy sources. Despite challenges in data integration, cybersecurity, and regulatory issues, the continued advancement of grid optimization will play a crucial role in ensuring the sustainability of modern electrical systems.

FAULT DIAGNOSIS IN ELECTRICAL MACHINES

Fault diagnosis in electrical machines is the process of identifying, analyzing, and locating faults or failures in the electrical, mechanical, or control systems of machinery such as motors, generators, transformers, and other electromechanical devices. These faults can be caused by various factors, including electrical imbalances, mechanical wear, environmental conditions, and operational stresses. Timely detection of faults and accurate diagnosis are crucial for minimizing downtime, preventing catastrophic failures, and optimizing the performance and longevity of electrical machines.

In industrial applications, electrical machines are often critical components, and any failure can lead to significant operational disruptions, loss of productivity, or even safety hazards. Therefore, fault diagnosis plays a vital role in predictive maintenance, energy management, and the overall reliability of electrical systems. It combines advanced monitoring techniques, signal processing, and diagnostic algorithms to identify the root causes of failures and recommend corrective actions.

Types of Faults in Electrical Machines

Electrical machines can experience a wide range of faults, which can be broadly categorized into electrical, mechanical, thermal, and control faults. Understanding these faults is essential for designing appropriate diagnostic strategies.

Electrical Faults

Electrical faults are caused by issues within the electrical circuits and components of the machine. These include:

- Short Circuits: Occur when electrical conductors come into contact with each other, causing a surge in current flow that may damage the insulation or windings.
- Open Circuits: Caused by broken wires or faulty connections, leading to a loss of power to part or all of the machine.
- Ground Faults: Occur when a live wire makes contact with the ground, causing leakage currents and potential safety hazards.
- Imbalanced Voltage or Current: Voltage imbalances can cause motors to overheat or run inefficiently, leading to premature wear.
- Insulation Failure: Breakdown of insulation materials over time, leading to short circuits or leakage currents.

Mechanical Faults

Mechanical faults in electrical machines are related to the physical moving parts of the machine, such as the rotor, bearings, and shafts. These faults include:

- Bearing Failures: Caused by insufficient lubrication, excessive load, or wear and tear, leading to vibrations and mechanical damage.

- Rotor Imbalance: Occurs when the rotor's weight distribution is uneven, causing vibrations and mechanical stress.
- Shaft Misalignment: Improper alignment of shafts can lead to increased friction, wear, and heat generation.
- Cavitation or Friction in Fans: The failure of cooling fans or improper airflow can result in overheating.

Thermal Faults

Thermal faults occur due to excessive heating of the electrical machine components, which can result in insulation damage, component degradation, and reduced operational efficiency. These faults include:

- Overheating of Windings: Due to excessive current, insufficient cooling, or poor heat dissipation.
- Thermal Runaway: A condition where increasing temperature causes the insulation to degrade, which further increases the heat, leading to a vicious cycle of overheating.

Control System Faults

Faults in the control systems of electrical machines can result in improper operation, leading to efficiency losses or even failures. These include:

- Faulty Sensors or Feedback Systems: Incorrect readings from sensors can lead to improper control actions, such as speed, position, or current control.
- Inverter Failures: Malfunctions in the inverter or drive control systems can cause issues like incorrect voltage levels, overloading, or unresponsive operation.
- Faulty Protection Systems: Failure of protective devices such as circuit breakers or relays can result in undetected faults or failure to disconnect the machine in case of a problem.

Fault Diagnosis Techniques

Various techniques and tools are used to detect and diagnose faults in electrical machines. These methods are typically based on analyzing electrical signals, mechanical vibrations, temperature, or a combination of these. The key techniques include:

a. Vibration Analysis

Vibration analysis is one of the most common methods for diagnosing mechanical faults in rotating machinery, such as motors and generators. It involves measuring the vibrations generated by the machine and analyzing the frequency spectrum to identify abnormalities that might indicate faults such as:

- Imbalance in the rotor.
- Bearing wear.
- Shaft misalignment.

Advanced vibration analysis tools utilize sensors like accelerometers and gyroscopes to detect variations in vibration patterns, which are then analyzed using signal processing techniques such as Fast Fourier Transform (FFT) to detect fault signatures.

b. Motor Current Signature Analysis (MCSA)

Motor Current Signature Analysis involves analyzing the electrical current drawn by an induction motor to detect faults. This method relies on the fact that different faults in an electrical machine result in distinct patterns of current distortion. For instance:

- Bearing defects often show up as high-frequency harmonics in the current.
- Rotor bar faults can result in sideband frequencies related to the operating speed of the machine.

MCSA is useful for detecting faults like broken rotor bars, stator winding faults, and bearing issues without the need for physical intervention.

c. Thermal Imaging

Thermal imaging uses infrared cameras to capture heat signatures from electrical machines. Anomalies such as hot spots on windings, bearings, or other components can indicate overheating, insulation breakdown, or mechanical friction. Thermal imaging is a non-invasive technique and is often used for routine maintenance to prevent equipment failures before they occur.

d. Acoustic Emission Monitoring

Acoustic emission monitoring is used to detect high-frequency sound waves generated by fault-related phenomena, such as cracks or material degradation. These emissions are captured by sensors placed on the machine's surface. Acoustic emissions are especially useful in detecting faults like insulation failure or cracks in structural components.

e. Signal Processing Techniques

Signal processing techniques, including time-domain and frequency-domain analysis, are employed to extract meaningful information from the electrical signals of the machine. Techniques like Fast Fourier Transform (FFT), wavelet analysis, and spectral analysis help identify fault signatures in the signals that are often not visible in standard current and voltage waveforms.

f. Artificial Intelligence and Machine Learning

Artificial intelligence (AI) and machine learning (ML) algorithms are increasingly used in fault diagnosis to automate the identification and prediction of faults. These algorithms can learn patterns from historical fault data and continuously improve their accuracy in diagnosing faults. AI-based systems use techniques such as:

- Neural Networks: To classify faults based on training data.
- Support Vector Machines (SVM): For pattern recognition and fault classification.
- Deep Learning: For more complex fault patterns and the identification of subtle fault indicators from large datasets.

These advanced diagnostic tools enable predictive maintenance, where potential faults can be detected and addressed before they result in machine failure.

Fault Diagnosis Process

The fault diagnosis process generally involves the following steps:

1. Data Acquisition: The first step involves collecting data from the machine using sensors like vibration sensors, temperature sensors, and current/voltage meters. Real-time data acquisition is crucial for accurate fault detection.
2. Signal Processing and Analysis: The collected data is processed using various signal processing techniques to extract features that indicate potential faults. Techniques like FFT, wavelet analysis, and pattern recognition are used to analyze the signals.
3. Fault Detection and Isolation: Based on the analysis, the system detects abnormalities and isolates the affected components. This step may involve the use of diagnostic models, AI algorithms, or pre-established fault signatures.
4. Fault Classification and Severity Assessment: After detecting the fault, the next step is to classify it (e.g., bearing fault, rotor imbalance) and assess its severity. Severity assessment helps prioritize maintenance actions.
5. Maintenance Decision and Remediation: Based on the diagnosis, the system recommends maintenance actions, such as repairs, replacements, or further monitoring. Predictive maintenance strategies may suggest corrective actions before the fault progresses to a critical stage.

Importance of Fault Diagnosis in Electrical Machines

The importance of fault diagnosis in electrical machines cannot be overstated. By detecting faults early, operators can prevent catastrophic failures, reduce downtime, and lower maintenance costs. Accurate fault diagnosis also ensures:

- Increased Equipment Lifespan: Timely maintenance helps prevent wear and tear on electrical machine components, extending their operational life.
- Enhanced Reliability and Safety: Identifying and fixing faults promptly enhances the overall reliability of the machine, preventing safety hazards and ensuring that the machinery operates within safe parameters.
- Cost Savings: Early fault detection reduces the need for expensive emergency repairs or machine replacements and improves resource allocation for maintenance tasks.

Fault diagnosis in electrical machines is a critical component of modern maintenance practices, especially in industrial settings where reliability and efficiency are paramount. By utilizing a combination of vibration analysis, current signature analysis, thermal imaging, and advanced signal processing techniques, electrical machine faults can be detected, analyzed, and addressed before they lead to major failures. Furthermore, the integration of AI and machine learning enhances the accuracy and predictive capabilities of fault diagnosis, enabling a more proactive approach to maintenance. Through early detection and remediation, fault diagnosis not only improves operational efficiency but also contributes to the overall safety, reliability, and cost-effectiveness of electrical systems.

ELEVEN

FUTURE TRENDS

AI-Driven Digital Twins represent the next evolution of digital twin technology, where the interaction between real-time data and AI algorithms leads to smarter, more autonomous decision-making processes. A Digital Twin is essentially a digital replica of a physical system or asset, but with the integration of AI, these twins can simulate not just the present state of the system but predict future behavior, automate operations, and continuously adapt to evolving conditions. AI algorithms, such as machine learning, deep learning, and neural networks, process vast amounts of data from IoT devices, sensors, and machine learning models to identify patterns, detect anomalies, and optimize performance. In industries such as manufacturing, energy, and healthcare, AI-driven Digital Twins can predict when equipment will fail, optimize energy usage, and even recommend design changes. This intelligence layer transforms a passive model into an active participant in the system, providing insights that are not just reactive but anticipatory. One of the key benefits of AI integration is predictive maintenance, where AI can forecast failures before they happen, saving on costs, increasing system uptime, and improving the overall reliability of physical assets. However, the adoption of AI in Digital Twins does present challenges such as the need for high-quality data, computational power, and the risk of model errors due to unforeseen conditions, making continuous refinement and oversight necessary. As the technology matures, AI-driven Digital Twins are poised to revolutionize industries by making systems smarter, more autonomous, and more efficient.

Blockchain technology has gained widespread attention due to its potential for secure, transparent, and decentralized data management. In the context of Digital Twins and IoT, Blockchain offers significant benefits in terms of ensuring secure data sharing, enabling trusted transactions, and safeguarding sensitive information. Digital Twins are inherently reliant on real-time data from connected devices, machines, and sensors. As this data is transmitted across various platforms and stakeholders, ensuring its integrity and security becomes a challenge. Blockchain, with its decentralized ledger system, can provide a reliable framework to track and record data exchanges between multiple parties without the need for a centralized authority. This ensures that the data cannot be tampered with or altered, thus guaranteeing its authenticity and traceability. For example, in industrial applications, Blockchain can be used to verify the authenticity of parts used in manufacturing processes, ensuring that only certified components are integrated into a product, which is critical in sectors like aerospace and automotive. Moreover, Blockchain's smart contract functionality can automate decision-making processes, enabling more efficient and secure operations. Additionally, blockchain can facilitate transparent, real-time transactions across the supply chain, such as payments or tracking inventory, without intermediary delays. Despite its promise, challenges such as scalability, energy consumption (especially with proof-of-work models), and regulatory hurdles remain as barriers to its widespread adoption in Digital Twins and secure data sharing.

The integration of Augmented Reality (AR) and Virtual Reality (VR) with Digital Twin technology offers an immersive, interactive, and intuitive interface for interacting with complex systems and assets. While Digital Twins create digital replicas of physical objects, systems, or environments, AR and VR enhance the user experience by providing a visual, spatial, and real-time representation of this data. AR overlays digital information onto the real-world environment, allowing users to interact with both the physical and digital worlds simultaneously. For instance, in a manufacturing plant, engineers can use AR to view real-time performance data of machines, identify potential faults, or get step-by-step maintenance instructions directly overlaid on the machine. On the other hand, VR allows users to step into entirely simulated environments, making it ideal for training, design, and simulation purposes. Engineers, for instance, can use VR to walk through a virtual factory floor or simulate troubleshooting procedures for complex machinery without risk to physical assets. This synergy between Digital Twins and AR/VR has vast implications in sectors like industrial maintenance, healthcare, real estate, and urban planning. However, challenges such as hardware limitations, the need for high-bandwidth data transmission, and user training need to be addressed for the effective integration of AR and VR with Digital Twins. When executed correctly, this integration not only improves operational efficiency but also enhances the safety, training, and design capabilities of industries, making complex tasks more manageable and actionable.

As the adoption of Digital Twin technology becomes more widespread across industries, the need for common standards and interoperability becomes increasingly critical. Interoperability refers to the ability of different systems, devices, and software platforms to communicate and exchange data seamlessly. In the realm of Digital Twins, interoperability ensures that data collected from various sources, such as IoT devices, sensors, and control systems, can be easily shared, integrated, and analyzed within a unified framework. Without standardized protocols, organizations may struggle with siloed systems that cannot exchange information, which undermines the potential of Digital Twins. Various industries have already begun efforts to establish standards, such as the Industrial Internet of Things (IIoT) and Open Platform Communications (OPC), to streamline communication between diverse devices and platforms. Additionally, standardized data formats like XML, JSON, and industry-specific standards like ISO/IEC 62264 for manufacturing operations ensure that the information shared is consistent, interpretable, and actionable. Furthermore, the standardization of security protocols is crucial to ensure that data exchanged across systems remains secure and complies with privacy regulations. While the development of common standards has made significant progress, challenges remain, particularly when integrating legacy systems with modern Digital Twin frameworks. Furthermore, there is a need for universal standards across diverse industries to ensure that Digital Twin technology can be universally applied and adopted across geographical boundaries and sectors. Addressing these interoperability challenges through collaborative industry efforts will unlock the full potential of Digital Twins, ensuring they can operate seamlessly across systems, enhance operational efficiency, and deliver optimal value.

TWELVE

CHALLENGES AND ETHICAL CONSIDERATIONS

Cybersecurity Risks and Mitigation

As the integration of Digital Twin technology into electrical engineering systems increases, so does the risk of cyber threats. Digital Twins, by their very nature, rely on continuous data flow and real-time updates between physical and virtual systems. This connectivity introduces numerous cybersecurity vulnerabilities, making these systems prime targets for cyber-attacks, data breaches, and malicious interference. For instance, hackers could potentially manipulate the digital replicas of electrical assets to disrupt power grids or plant operations, leading to catastrophic consequences such as system failures or even physical damage to electrical infrastructure.

The cybersecurity risks associated with Digital Twin technology are multifaceted. First, the vast amount of data transmitted between physical assets and digital models creates potential entry points for cybercriminals. Second, the complexity of interconnected systems means that a vulnerability in one component can compromise the entire system. Additionally, the lack of standardized security protocols across industries makes it challenging to create robust defense mechanisms for these systems.

To mitigate these risks, a multi-layered security approach is necessary. This includes encrypting data in transit and at rest, implementing stringent access controls, and using advanced authentication methods such as biometrics or multi-factor authentication to ensure that only authorized personnel can access critical systems. Furthermore, regular security audits, penetration testing, and the use of firewalls and intrusion detection systems are vital for identifying and mitigating potential threats before they escalate. It is also essential to develop a security culture within organizations, where employees are continuously trained on cybersecurity best practices and potential threats.

As Digital Twin technology evolves, so must the strategies to safeguard it. Collaboration between industry stakeholders, cybersecurity experts, and regulatory bodies is essential to develop security standards tailored to the unique needs of digital models in electrical systems. Proactive cybersecurity measures and constant vigilance will be key to minimizing the risks associated with the digitalization of electrical assets.

Data Privacy and Ownership

With the proliferation of Internet of Things (IoT) devices and sensors, Digital Twin systems rely heavily on vast amounts of real-time data to function. This data often includes sensitive information about electrical infrastructure, operational behaviors, and performance metrics. As such, data privacy and ownership become critical issues in the deployment and utilization of Digital Twins.

Data privacy concerns arise from the fact that Digital Twin systems are designed to track and monitor every aspect of an electrical system, which often includes operational data that could be deemed sensitive. For instance, in power grids, Digital Twins collect data on the flow of electricity, load management, and other sensitive operational details that could be exploited by malicious actors if not properly protected. Additionally, if the data is mishandled or improperly shared, it could lead to privacy violations or the unintentional disclosure of confidential business strategies or customer information.

The issue of data ownership is equally complex. As Digital Twin systems rely on data generated by various sources, including IoT devices, sensors, and third-party systems, the question arises: who owns the data collected by these systems? Is it the company that owns the physical assets, the third-party data providers, or the operators using the digital model for optimization and monitoring? The challenge of clearly defining data ownership becomes even more significant when considering the complexities of cloud storage and data sharing, where the digital assets of multiple parties may be involved.

To address these challenges, organizations must implement clear data governance policies. This includes defining who owns the data, how it will be stored, and who has access to it. Data encryption techniques should be employed to safeguard sensitive information and ensure that data is only accessible by authorized personnel. Additionally, organizations must comply with data protection laws such as the General Data Protection Regulation (GDPR) in Europe, which outlines strict guidelines for the collection, processing, and sharing of personal data. Furthermore, the implementation of data anonymization techniques can help mitigate privacy risks by ensuring that individual identifiers are not easily traceable to specific users or systems.

Clear contracts and agreements between stakeholders involved in data sharing, as well as transparent data policies, will be key to managing ownership disputes and ensuring compliance with privacy regulations. As Digital Twin technology becomes more widespread, it will be imperative to establish international standards for data privacy and ownership in the electrical engineering sector.

Reliability and Accuracy of Digital Twins

The effectiveness of a Digital Twin system depends heavily on the reliability and accuracy of its virtual model. Since Digital Twins simulate real-world systems in a virtual environment, any discrepancies between the digital model and the actual physical system can lead to incorrect decision-making, reduced performance, or even system failure. For instance, if the Digital Twin of a power grid is not accurately reflecting the status of the physical grid, decisions made based on the model, such as fault detection or energy distribution, could be detrimental.

The accuracy of Digital Twins is influenced by several factors, including the quality of the data being fed into the system, the complexity of the model, and the algorithms used to simulate real-world behavior. High-quality, real-time data is essential for creating an accurate digital representation, and discrepancies in data can lead to inaccurate predictions or flawed simulations. For example, outdated sensor data or inaccurate sensor readings can affect the digital replica's performance, leading to incorrect fault diagnoses or inappropriate responses to operational changes.

Ensuring the reliability and accuracy of Digital Twins requires continuous calibration and validation against real-world data. This process involves regularly comparing the outputs of the digital model with actual system performance and making necessary adjustments to improve the model's predictive power. Advanced machine learning and AI techniques can also be employed to refine and improve the accuracy of Digital Twins over time by learning from historical data and predicting potential future behaviors. Additionally, regular system checks and real-time monitoring of both physical and digital assets will ensure that the Digital Twin remains accurate and reflects the true state of the physical system.

As Digital Twins are integrated into more critical systems, their accuracy becomes even more important. For example, in electrical grids, the consequences of inaccurate models can be severe, potentially leading to power outages, equipment damage, or safety hazards. Therefore, establishing industry standards for model validation, accuracy testing, and continuous improvement will be crucial in ensuring the reliability of Digital Twin systems.

Regulatory and Compliance Issues

As Digital Twin technology becomes more widespread in industries such as electrical engineering, regulatory and compliance issues take on a critical role. The integration of Digital Twins involves not just technology, but also the management of large volumes of data and complex interactions between physical assets and virtual systems. This brings forward numerous challenges in ensuring that Digital Twin systems comply with industry-specific regulations and standards, as well as broader legal frameworks regarding data protection, privacy, and safety.

In the context of electrical engineering, regulatory requirements often focus on ensuring the safety, reliability, and security of energy infrastructure. Digital Twin systems, particularly those used to monitor and control power grids, must adhere to strict safety standards to prevent failures that could lead to blackouts, equipment damage, or even safety hazards. These regulations are designed to ensure that electrical systems are operated within safe parameters and that potential faults or issues are detected early enough to mitigate risks.

Compliance with data protection and privacy laws is another key consideration, especially when Digital Twins are handling sensitive operational data. Regulations such as the GDPR in Europe or the California Consumer Privacy Act (CCPA) in the United States mandate strict guidelines for how personal and sensitive data is collected, stored, and shared. For Digital Twins, this could mean ensuring that the data used to model systems does not violate privacy rights or expose confidential business information.

In addition, industry-specific standards for interoperability and system integration must be followed to ensure that Digital Twins can be integrated with existing infrastructure and communication systems without compromising their effectiveness or security. These standards help ensure that different systems can communicate effectively and that data can be exchanged seamlessly across platforms and devices, reducing the risk of errors or incompatibilities.

To navigate these challenges, organizations must work closely with regulatory bodies, industry groups, and legal advisors to develop strategies for ensuring compliance with all relevant regulations. It is essential to stay up to date with evolving legal frameworks and to build compliance into the design, development, and deployment phases of Digital Twin systems. By doing so, organizations can ensure that their use of Digital Twin technology not only enhances efficiency and reliability but also adheres to legal and ethical standards.

THIRTEEN
CONCLUSION

In the rapidly evolving landscape of electrical engineering, integrating advanced digital technologies is reshaping how systems are designed, monitored, and managed. One of the most transformative concepts emerging in this field is the Digital Twin technology, which has rapidly advanced from a theoretical idea to a core element of modern electrical systems. The Digital Twin, a dynamic virtual replica of a physical system, process, or asset, acts as a real-time simulation that reflects its real-world counterpart's actual behavior, status, and operational parameters. Initially conceptualized in industries such as aerospace and manufacturing, the application of Digital Twin technology in electrical engineering is proving to be a game-changer. It enables engineers and operators to virtually replicate complex electrical systems, such as power grids, energy distribution networks, and electrical machines, and monitor them in real time. This advancement allows for not only an unprecedented level of understanding but also control and optimization of electrical systems. By leveraging data collected from IoT devices, sensors, and other data sources, Digital Twins can simulate real-world conditions and make predictions regarding system performance, fault occurrence, and maintenance needs. These capabilities allow for a shift from traditional, reactive maintenance practices to proactive strategies, including predictive maintenance, fault diagnosis, and optimized resource allocation. As the demand for energy increases globally and electrical systems become more complex and interconnected, the need for more efficient, reliable, and intelligent management solutions becomes critical. Digital Twin technology offers the potential to significantly reduce downtime, enhance operational efficiency, and minimize operational costs by simulating and analyzing various scenarios in a virtual environment before making decisions in the physical world. However, while the advantages are clear, the journey from conceptualization to implementation involves numerous challenges, ranging from technical hurdles in data integration and system interoperability to the complexities of cybersecurity and real-time monitoring. In order to unlock the full potential of Digital Twins, substantial investment in research, development, and industry collaboration is required. As industries continue to evolve and embrace digitalization, the role of Digital Twins in electrical engineering is poised to expand, offering smarter, more sustainable solutions for energy generation, transmission, and consumption. This paper explores the multifaceted journey of Digital Twin technology in the context of electrical engineering, examining its evolution, applications, challenges, and strategies for successful implementation. From the conceptualization of the idea to the real-world integration of Digital Twins into electrical systems, this work seeks to provide an in-depth analysis of how this technology is transforming electrical engineering practices and reshaping the future of smart energy management. The integration of Digital Twins in the electrical sector is not only a technological innovation but a vital step towards achieving the goals of sustainability, efficiency, and resilience in the face of an increasingly complex and interconnected energy landscape. This paper provides a comprehensive exploration of these advancements, detailing the current state of Digital Twin technology and envisioning its future impact on electrical systems worldwide. Through case studies, application examples, and industry insights, we will delve deeper into how Digital Twins are driving smarter decision-making, optimizing system performance, and contributing to a more sustainable and secure energy future. The transition from concept to practical implementation in electrical engineering, while challenging, is pivotal in realizing the potential of Digital Twin technology in creating intelligent, responsive, and sustainable electrical systems for the future.

In conclusion, Digital Twin technology stands as a transformative force within the field of electrical engineering, offering a wealth of opportunities to enhance system design, operation, and maintenance. By creating virtual replicas of physical assets, Digital Twins enable real-time monitoring, predictive maintenance, optimization, and fault diagnosis, which collectively contribute to more efficient, reliable, and sustainable electrical systems. The integration of this technology into power grids, renewable energy systems, electrical machines, and other critical infrastructure holds immense potential for revolutionizing the way we manage energy resources. While significant progress has been made in applying Digital Twin concepts, challenges remain in terms of data integration, interoperability, cybersecurity, and ensuring seamless real-world implementation. Nonetheless, as technological advancements continue to evolve and industries increasingly adopt digitalization strategies, the role of Digital Twins in electrical engineering will only grow more prominent. By overcoming current obstacles and fostering collaboration between industry, academia, and technology providers, the future of Digital Twins promises to create smarter, more resilient electrical systems that can meet the demands of an interconnected and increasingly complex global energy landscape. The path from concept to implementation is intricate, but the promise of Digital Twins driving efficiency, sustainability, and innovation in electrical engineering is undeniable, marking a critical step towards the future of intelligent energy management.

* 9 7 9 8 8 9 9 0 6 7 0 4 4 *